LOOTENS ON
PHOTOGRAPHIC ENLARGING
AND PRINT QUALITY

Lootens ON

by
Ghislain Lootens F.P.S.A., F.R.P.S.
—all photographs by the author—

BALTIMORE, MARYLAND
The Camera

HOTOGRAPHIC ENLARGING
and PRINT QUALITY

Set and printed by Fleet-McGinley, Inc.
at Baltimore, Md., United States of
America.

Made in U. S. A.

To

JOHN S. ROWAN

without whose friendly persistence and encouragement this book never would have been written.

DEDICATION   *J. Ghislain Lootens, F.P.S.A., F.R.P.*

FOREWORD

THE first thing that every aspiring photographer should learn, and that every experienced hand should never forget, is that NOBODY ever made a picture which EVERYONE liked. That is simply impossible to accomplish because we are all individuals with definite likes or dislikes and some will always like certain things better than others, whether they be pictures of machines, dogs, landscapes, or portrait studies. Even on the question of what is perfect technique there is ground for disagreement. Some people, for example, shudder at seeing a brilliant, glossy print showing fine detail, while others practically have a convulsion when a diffused, grainy picture printed on a buff stock is put in front of them.

When we try to analyze what it really all amounts to, we come down to a single denominator—we should all be able to make the kind of pictures which *we* personally like and exactly in the manner in which *we* like them. By this I mean we should cultivate a technique which will give us, as individuals, such perfect control over our material that we can always get into the final print exactly what we desire. If we can do that, we can become either a successful amateur or a successful professional. This, of course, is another way of saying that a photographer must be a perfect craftsman if he wants to get the best out of his hobby or his profession.

I believe it was Renoir who, more than 60 years ago, when speaking about painting, made the remark, "Today everybody seems to be a genius, but nobody can draw a hand anymore." He was pleading for better craftsmanship in the medium of painting. Very often there is a tendency to overlook the fact that behind every good picture there must be expert craftsmanship. Sometimes a photographer may get an opportunity to photograph wonderful subject material and his picture may be a success just because of that alone. But how much more satisfying it would be if, in addition to the fine subject material, there also was good craftsmanship.

This book, therefore, is intended to show the average photographer how to acquire a method of using photography in such a way that he will *be able to put into his prints that which he personally desires*. Many of the pictures selected for this book have been picked more particularly to show the possibilities of photography than for any other reason, and it is hoped that you will be encouraged, either to go out and take better pictures or else make a thorough search through your old files to see if some previously discarded negative can't be resurrected and made into something to please you.

Above all, don't be one of those who learns everything so quickly that you never really learn anything well. Do not expect miracles right away. Take hundreds of negatives; make hundreds of prints and then the results will begin to mean something to you.

J. GHISLAIN LOOTENS

TABLE OF CONTENTS

CONTENTS *Continued*

CHAPTER I

IN THE BEGINNING ---

HOW TO GET THE PROPER NEGATIVE

THE greatest thrill in the life of the average photographer is unquestionably the day when he makes his first enlargement, yet he strives after that to make things more complicated for himself.

Let us assume that your photography is easily improved if you have a regular method of working, and that *what you know* is not so important as *how well* you can do a certain thing. The shortest cut to developing a system is to bring it down to the bare essentials. Right from the start let me suggest that four things will get the system working for you in the shortest possible time. First, stick to one developer, one film, one type of paper, one enlarger—and even one camera. To those of you who are just beginning photography, please stick to such a system for at least six months. And those who have been fumbling for the last few years, please start all over again and give it a trial. Sticking to one thing until you have mastered it will not only make your photography more fun and more successful but it will eliminate much waste of materials and money.

One of the greatest mistakes so many of our enthusiasts make is continually attempting to test a film, a paper or developer. Very few amateurs and even professionals have adequate knowledge and the right darkroom to be able to really test anything efficiently. Rather let us take for granted the fact that the materials we buy in the stores are perfectly tested and suited to our needs. The more you work in photography, the more you realize that the secret of good work does not lie in any particular paper or tricky formula, but rather in the knowledge you have gained working in one simple manner.

Let me assure you that when you go into a store and buy a certain brand of film, paper or developer, it will be quite suitable for your work if you really understand it. Here, too, let me remind you that I am not trying to discourage you from experimenting, but asking that you postpone it until you have acquired such a good system that you really have something to compare. It is extremely difficult to decide whether one thing is actually better than another unless you have, through experience and judgment, acquired sufficient knowledge to be able to make an intelligent decision.

How do we start on our system? One of the first things we learn when we begin to study photography is that a good negative is of prime importance. Photography is a real pleasure when we have a good negative. You don't have to be an expert to make a good print under such conditions, but it takes a wizard to make a good picture from a bad negative. The question then follows—what is a good negative? Here, too, you may often be confused, for if you approach a dozen friends you may find that each has a different idea on the subject. Some like a thin negative, some a medium—and still others a heavy one. Then there is still a difference as to how thin, how medium and how heavy. Later you will hear such confusing terms as contrast, brilliance, scale, etc.—things which often frighten away the beginner and confuse even many an advanced amateur.

GETTING A GOOD NEGATIVE

For many years past I have been teaching what I consider an almost fool-proof system for getting, if not a perfect, at least a very usable negative, no matter under what conditions it might have been taken. Throughout the years I have seen students coming back with pictures taken during their travels in all sorts of lands and all kinds of climes which have been keen disappointments instead of fine shots. In trying to insure at least one good negative from each desirable scene, and with the least effort or resort to science, I have been insisting that *three negatives* should be taken of *each scene*. The first negative, naturally, should always be as normally exposed as can be figured out either by the use of a meter or by the experience of the photographer. The second negative should always be *four times* over-exposed, and the third negative *four times* under-exposed. Please

2

note when I say four times that I do not mean two times. With present-day films there is not much sense in merely changing the exposure by one stop. If you really want to see a difference you must go two stops. Of course, this variation in exposure can be manipulated by either the lens stop or the shutter speed or both, whatever seems best at the time of picture taking. But by having these three negatives, you practically insure yourself against any kind of disappointment later on.

For example, no matter whether your exposure meter was in good working condition or not, regardless of whether the emulsion speed of your film was correct, or no matter how careless the development may have been, one of those negatives simply has to be pretty good and quite usable. I do not intend to say this is the most scientific manner of doing things, but I do know it is something that everyone should do who wants to have a guaranteed picture which has to be made under uncontrollable lighting conditions or in unusual places.

DEVELOPING THE FILM

In most of these instances, if you do your developing yourself, develop for the normal time, however, if you have a way of segregating your roll-film or film pack so you can make notations as to whether the pictures were taken under flat or contrasty lighting conditions on each roll or pack, you then have much further control to insure the theoretically perfect negative. As we undoubtedly all remember, normal developing times apply only to pictures taken where the *lighting conditions* are also *normal,* or in other words where the light ratio between highlights and shadows runs approximately 1 to 4. If the contrast between lights and shadows is greater than 1 to 4 we should develop for *less* time than the normal developing time, and if the contrasts should be less than 1 to 4, then we should develop for a *longer* time than normal. Or, to put it more plainly, the only time that normal developing time should be used is when we have normal lighting—when we have contrasty lighting we should under-develop our negatives, and when we have flat lighting conditions we should over-develop the negatives.

If you find that most of your negatives print a bit flat or muddy on your brand of No. 2 paper but do appear better on the No. 3 grade, it is an indication you need to *increase* your negative developing time. Sometimes an increase of 10 to 25% over the indicated normal time is necessary. We must remember that the "normal" developing time

3

suggested by the manufacturer of a film or developer is not a sacrosanct declaration. In a sense it is only a guidepost—an averaging of many conditions—YOU are the only one who can decide what kind of negative you need.

If, on the other hand, your present negatives print best on No. 1 grade (soft) paper, then decrease the developing time. In my experience, I have found that most amateurs *under-develop* their negatives and therefore find it difficult to get the much desired pep and quality in their prints.

The density of a negative does not determine its contrast. A negative may be thin (transparent) but very contrasty or it can be dense (opaque) and extremely flat. The density of a negative will determine its printing time—a thin negative naturally requires a shorter exposure time than a dense one, regardless of the paper used.

Under normal conditions, try to get negatives which are neither too thin nor too dense. This you can guarantee by using the "3 exposure" method outlined above. The contrast of these negatives is also in your hands because you must pick the proper developing time.

If you keep in mind the idea of taking three negatives to get a correct exposure and the variations possible by altering the developing times for different contrasts of lighting, you will acquire in a *practical* sense, the most important elements of making good negatives, in the shortest possible time.

CHAPTER II

THE ENLARGER

THE kind of negative you will require to get the best possible prints will depend upon several factors which have nothing to do with the actual picture itself but which will be determined by the equipment and materials you possess. The first important thing to influence your negative is the type of enlarger which you use. You must realize that enlarging, especially when a condenser enlarger is used, *increases* the contrast of the negative. That is quite often overlooked by a photographer when he makes a contact print from a negative which looks fairly normal, and then resorts to the enlarging process and finds his negative has been thrown out of scale.

The *type* of enlarger which we intend to use really has a tremendous influence on the type of negative we need, much more than is generally realized. In a general sense there are three types of enlargers which should be considered, although among these three types we have many variations. The first type of enlarger is the diffusion enlarger, one which uses either Cooper Hewitt or fluorescent lighting, or a frosted or opal bulb in a reflector with perhaps an opal or ground glass as a means of further diffusing the light before it reaches the negative. Such an enlarger requires, comparatively, a strong negative, a negative which practically resembles the contrast of one used for contact printing. If the average "weak" negative, so much admired by many fine-grain workers, is placed in a diffusing enlarger or any of the above types and printed on a normal grade of paper, there is apt to be great disappointment, the resulting picture being too flat and without brilliance.

The other extreme from the diffusion enlarger, is the pure condenser enlarging system which utilizes a clear projection bulb and a set of two condensers to collect the light and to project it through the negative. This type of enlarger gives such a contrasty light that the negative should be much softer and flatter in contrast than the one used for the diffusing type. These two types of enlargers, the diffusion and straight condenser types, are so far apart in the form of light which they give forth that they can make as much and even more difference in contrast than one grade of paper.

THE SEMI-DIFFUSION ENLARGER

In between these two extreme types comes the semi-diffusion enlarger which covers the following types of lighting systems: 1—a diffusion bulb and condensers, or, 2—a diffusion bulb with either a diffusing glass over the condensers or else one of the condensers itself acting as a diffuser. This semi-diffusion enlarger is, therefore, a compromise which tries to utilize the advantages of the diffusion enlarger (lack of harshness and absence of dust and grain-faults) and at the same time makes use of a condenser system so that we will have the speed and uniformity of light which we find with the strict condenser system. Naturally a negative best suited for this type of semi-diffusion enlarger should be one whose contrast falls between the two extremes.

To sum up: In enlarging, the use of a soft light or a hard light will have a great influence on the type of print which you will get from any given negative.

It is safe to assume that the typical enlarger of today is one which could be classified as a modified condenser enlarger, that is, with an opal bulb furnishing the light and with or without the glass diffusing screen placed immediately above the condensers, as is shown in Diagram 1. In some enlargers the condensers themselves act as a further diffuser, usually the top surface of the upper lens being ground to diffuse the light.

The modified condenser enlarger can be considered as very efficient and is extremely suitable for the smaller sized negatives, from 35 mm. up to $2\frac{1}{4}$ x $3\frac{1}{4}$. There is no reason, however, why it could not be used for the larger film sizes too, although it is not quite as necessary for the larger films.

Supporting Post:—This may be a single column, as is shown, or be of different design. The prime requisite is that it be strong and firmly attached to the base. As it carries the entire weight of the enlarger head, its rigidity will determine how much vibration can take place. Passing trucks or trains will induce a certain amount of shake in the instrument which, if past allowable limits, will spoil print definition.

Support Arm Bearing Surface: — This slides on the upright column and usually is equipped with a locking wheel which, when tightened, firmly holds the enlarger head in the desired position. On some models the vertical movement is secured by means of a hand-wheel, with a separate wheel for locking and on others the weight of the assembly is counterbalanced either with a sliding weight or a spring mechanism and the bearing moved easily by hand.

Angle Adjustment: — Many models incorporate this feature which allows the enlarger head to be swung at an angle to the base. The locking wheel is placed as shown and on some machines a graduated circle is supplied which enables the operator to reset the angle to any desired number of degrees from the vertical. The angular setting permits the enlarger to be used for correcting bad perspective in the negative or to exaggerate the perspective of a normal negative (Diagram 5).

The Lamp House:—Lamphouses vary in size and shape, according to the manufacturer's design. They should have adequate ventilation to keep the heat of the lamp from damaging the negative and should not permit too much light leakage. The lamp houses of models employing condensing lenses are usually of relatively small diameter, while those on enlargers employing the diffusion principle may be larger, to permit concentration of more light on the diffusing glass.

As it is essential that the lamp be located properly, to avoid a "hot spot" and provide even illumination over the entire negative, some models are provided with adjusting screws for centering the socket which holds the lamp. Other machines lacking this feature are aligned when they leave the factory and, so long as the standard bulb is used, will remain optically correct. This is of greater importance in the condenser type of enlarger than in any other.

The light bulb may be clear with a concentrated filament, as in the case of some condenser enlargers, or may be an opal bulb which provides diffused light for the semi-diffusion and diffusion types of enlargers.

The Optical System :—This consists of the lamp, diffusing screen and/or condenser and the lens, all of which should be kept in first class condition always. (See Diagram 2).

Negative Carrier :—The negative carrier lies immediately below the condensers and may be of the glass-less type, consisting of two smooth polished plates, that hold the negative in place over the opening through which the light passes. The type using glass has two glass plates between which the negative is clamped. Either type will work satisfactorily although there is more difficulty in keeping dust off the glass but this disadvantage may be counterbalanced by the fact that the glass-less type is not always satisfactory for large negatives as it sometimes permits them to buckle when heated by the lamp, thus throwing part of the image out of focus.

Bellows :—These provide the connecting link between the negative carrier and the lensboard. They may be the conventional leather bellows or a type made of metal, wherein one tube slides inside another. The bellows allow movement of the lens for focusing, which movement is accomplished by turning the focusing knob. It is important that the lensboard remains in any position to which it is adjusted, without slippage which will throw the image out of focus, perhaps during exposure. Friction drives should be firm, but not too tight and rack and pinion arrangements should not be allowed to become too worn before being repaired.

Lensboard :—In many enlargers the lensboard is removable to permit a quick change of lenses. The lensboard must be parallel to the negative and the easel surface, unless, of course, it is deliberately tilted.

The Lens :—As in a camera, the lens is the heart of the instrument and should be of high quality, reasonably fast and with good definition. Buy as good a lens as your budget will allow—there is not much sense in spending a fair sum of money for a good camera only to nullify this by using an inferior lens with the enlarger.

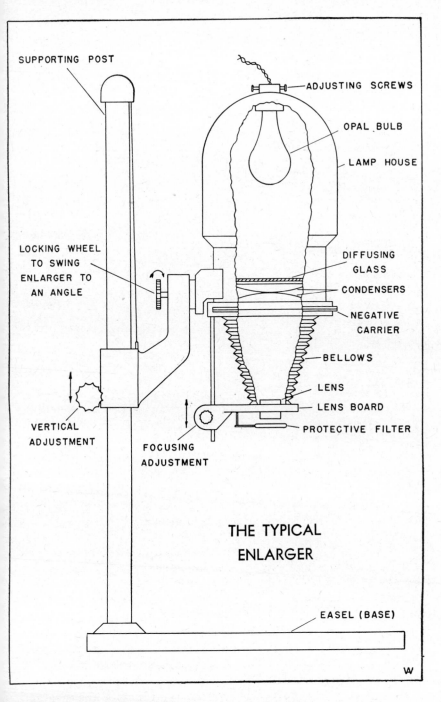

SUPPORTING POST

ADJUSTING SCREWS

OPAL BULB

LAMP HOUSE

LOCKING WHEEL
TO SWING
ENLARGER TO
AN ANGLE

DIFFUSING
GLASS

CONDENSERS

NEGATIVE
CARRIER

BELLOWS

LENS

LENS BOARD

PROTECTIVE FILTER

VERTICAL
ADJUSTMENT

FOCUSING
ADJUSTMENT

THE TYPICAL
ENLARGER

EASEL (BASE)

W

Diagram 1

9

The Protective Filter:—This is usually a red glass or plastic filter which can be swung into position below the lens to prevent the white light from reaching the paper while it is being placed in position. Many of these red filters are of too deep a color and can advantageously be replaced with an orange filter which will permit more light to come through for better vision and at the same time fully protect the paper.

No matter what the construction of the enlarger, there is one cardinal principle which applies to the proper functioning of all of them and that is, *they should be kept clean.* The lens should be wiped periodically with lens tissue and the whole machine taken down and cleaned to remove accumulated dust. A half hour spent cleaning the enlarger will save many hours spotting prints.

ENLARGER LIGHTING SYSTEMS

The lighting systems used in modern enlargers can be grouped into three distinct classes: The straight condenser system, shown in Diagram 2, Figure 1, the semi-diffused, Figure 2 and the diffused, Figures 3 and 4.

The straight condenser enlarger has a point light source and undiffused condensers which concentrate and focus the light rays to get the greatest efficiency.

An enlarger of this type requires fairly soft negatives in order to be able to use No. 2 papers to the best advantage. Under normal conditions, such an enlarger will have the effect of making the negative print one grade harder than if the same negative were placed in the enlarger shown in Figure 3. In other words, if a negative placed in a condenser enlarger, such as the one shown, would print exactly right on No. 1 (soft) paper, that same negative would give its best quality, when placed in the diffusion enlarger, if used in conjunction with No. 2 paper.

This, of course, does not mean that any particular type of enlarger is either efficient or inefficient but does prove that it is necessary for the worker to develop his negatives to fit the equipment— whether his enlarger is a condenser, semi-diffusion or diffusion type.

Figure 2 is the semi-diffused, modified system in which con-

10

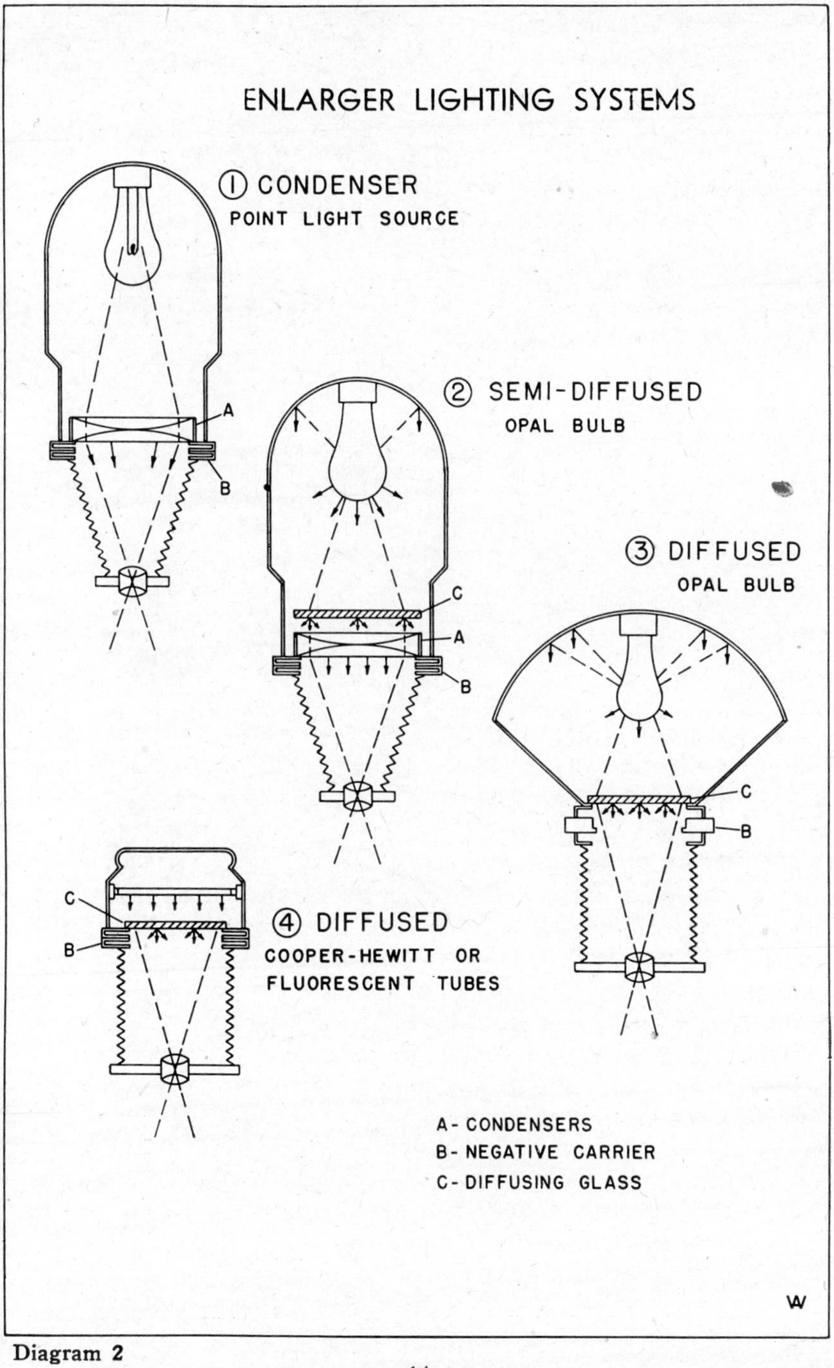
ENLARGER LIGHTING SYSTEMS
① CONDENSER
POINT LIGHT SOURCE
A
B
② SEMI-DIFFUSED
OPAL BULB
C
A
B
③ DIFFUSED
OPAL BULB
C
B
C
B
④ DIFFUSED
COOPER-HEWITT OR
FLUORESCENT TUBES
A- CONDENSERS
B- NEGATIVE CARRIER
C- DIFFUSING GLASS
W

Diagram 2

densers are used to get the maximum efficiency from the light, but their output is slightly softened through the use of a diffusing glass above the condensers or a diffuser incorporated in the top condenser.

In addition, instead of using a clear projection bulb, as in the straight condenser enlarger, an opal or frosted bulb is used as the light source, this too having the effect of cutting down the contrast. This type of enlarger, as far as its contrast is concerned, falls somewhere between the strong contrast of the enlarger in Figure 1 and the softer qualities of the enlarger shown in Figure 3. An enlarger of this type, while increasing the contrast in the negative more than in the case of a straight diffusion enlarger, is of course, not as drastic as the straight condenser type.

The diffusion enlarger, Figure 3, has a frosted or opal bulb and is used without condensers, evenness of light being obtained by placing one or more layers of diffusing glass above the negative itself. These enlargers are very suitable for those who have large negatives, from

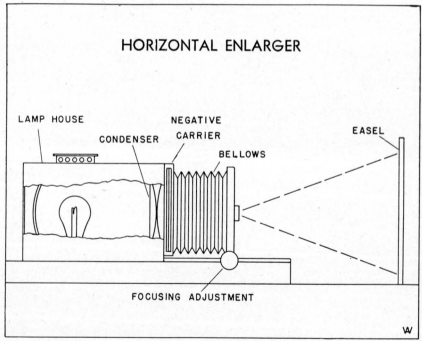

Diagram 3

3¼ x 4¼ up to 8 x 10, and are most popular with portrait studios as they minimize grain and retouching marks. For that type of work they are unexcelled.

Figure 4 also shows a diffusion type of enlarger but in this case fluorescent or mercury vapor tubes are used to provide the light. These are arranged in a zig-zag pattern above the diffusing glass screen, which insures even lighting over the whole field. As the light produced is "cold" there is no danger of overheating the negatives by prolonged exposure times. Some of the most efficient and mechanically perfect, but expensive, machines are available in this type of enlarger.

HORIZONTAL ENLARGER

Years ago, most of the enlargers were of the horizontal type but the necessity for conserving space in modern apartments has gradually made it lose favor. Essentially it is the same as the vertical enlarger, with the same movements. It is still a favorite with engravers and copyists but for home use it takes up much more room than the vertical type and has the further disadvantage that the paper must be attached to a vertical easel. (Diagram 3.)

However, the horizontal enlarger will turn out just as good work as any other kind, its disadvantages merely making it a bit more bothersome to operate. The enlarger shown is of the condenser type.

MAKING LARGER-THAN-ORDINARY PRINTS

Diagram 4 shows how you can make your enlarger give you bigger prints without having to resort to another focal length lens, by simply turning the enlarger around so that the projection can be made on the floor or in some cases, if the enlarger is adaptable, you can project directly on the wall in a horizontal position. Of course, in the latter case the size of the enlargement is only limited by your distance away from the wall, the same as when projecting slides or movies on a screen. When the enlarger is swung in either of these positions, it will be found advisable to clamp the baseboard to the table to prevent the whole assembly from becoming unbalanced and perhaps crashing to the floor.

In the event that the enlarger throw is too great, that is, the picture size is greater than you want it, even with the enlarger in the

13

lowest position on the post, block up the easel from the floor until the correct size is obtained. The easel may be placed on a box or chair to accomplish this.

When using the enlarger in a horizontal position, be sure that it is at right angles to the post. Most enlargers either have a graduated circle or are otherwise marked so that they may be placed quickly and true in the horizontal position. If the enlarger is out of line with the plane of the easel, distortion of the image will result. The paper may be held in position on the wall by means of push pins or bits of adhesive tape, if it is not convenient to rig up a vertical easel.

If you have a "so-called" portrait attachment for your single bellows camera—the simple lens which you slip over the regular camera lens for working close to the subject—see if it, or a similar lens, will fit over the lens on your enlarger. You will be happily surprised at the increased size of the projected image, after it has been refocused. It is usually desirable to stop down one or two extra stops to insure sharpness.

DISTORTION AND ITS CORRECTION

The enlarging process offers excellent opportunities to correct distortion which may be present in the original negative and which cannot be corrected by other means.

The distortion is frequently encountered in commercial work where the photographer is called upon to reproduce packaged products and other objects and in which the lines of the subject must be maintained in their true relationship. Even with a modern swing back camera it may not be possible exactly to meet the demands so further correction can be had during enlarging.

In architectural photography, where building lines must be kept true, the distortion occasioned by camera tilt can also be eliminated when making the print.

Diagram 5 shows four ways in which the image may be altered to suit the photographer. As you will note, all the methods are based upon tilting one part or another so that the projection distance from one side of the negative is increased. When a straight print is made in the normal manner, the negative is, or should be, absolutely parallel to

14

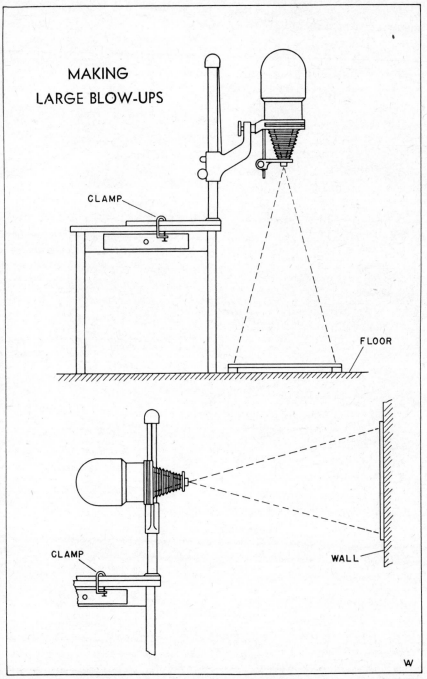

MAKING LARGE BLOW-UPS

CLAMP

FLOOR

CLAMP

WALL

W

Diagram 4

15

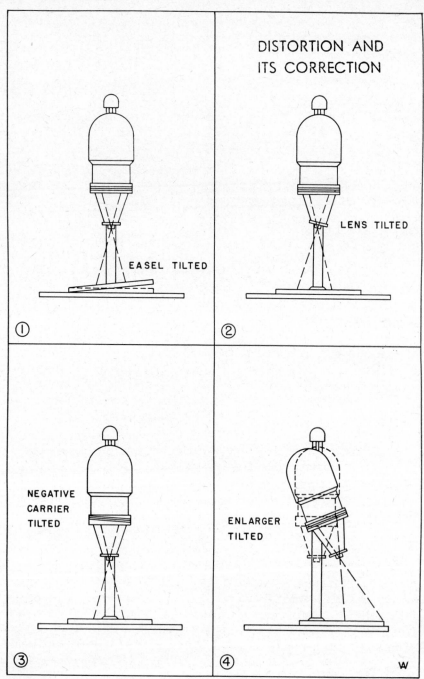

DISTORTION AND ITS CORRECTION

EASEL TILTED

LENS TILTED

NEGATIVE CARRIER TILTED

ENLARGER TILTED

① ② ③ ④

W

Diagram 5

the paper on the easel. Being parallel, each point receives the same degree of magnification and the print is, therefore, a true replica of the negative.

In Figure 1 of the diagram the easel has been tilted by raising one side. This may be accomplished by blocking up the end or, some easels are equipped with a ball and socket joint, similar to that found on tripods, which permits the easel to be placed in almost any position.

In this position, one leg of the projected image is shorter than the other and thus does not receive as great magnification. But, being nearer the lens the short side receives more light and hence during the exposure some dodging must be done to secure the same tone quality over the entire print.

In Figure 2 another means of accomplishing the same end is shown; however, not every enlarger is equipped with a tilting lensboard such as this and for those who do not have this equipment, the first method is advised.

Figure 3 shows yet another way of altering the lines of the image. Here, the negative has been tilted in relation to the lens and the same effect is achieved. This is similar to the swing back found on some cameras in its effect, and the tilting lensboard gives the same result in enlarging as tilting the camera lens when the picture is taken.

In Figure 4, the whole enlarger assembly has been swung from the vertical, achieving the same result as Figure 1. While many enlargers can be swung at an angle this way, some cannot, and in such cases, the first method should be used. When the machine is at an angle, the baseboard must be moved over to receive the image.

In addition to rectifying distortion present in the negative, in order to get correct perspective in the print, the same tiltings of easel, lens, negative carrier or baseboard may be used to distort the image. Caricatures of persons can easily be created by printing a normal portrait negative in this fashion. However, in serious portrait work, a *slight* amount of distortion will work wonders in slenderizing a heavy subject and it is particularly helpful in making a full faced individual appear to have a narrower and longer skull structure. This trick alone will sometimes save hours of retouching.

CHAPTER III

CHOOSING THE RIGHT PAPER FOR THE NEGATIVE

Another important factor which will determine the type of negative you desire is the *kind* of paper which you intend to use. Generally, we can classify papers as falling within three types—bromides, chloro-bromides, and chlorides.

Bromide papers are very fast enlarging papers which give very good cold-black tones but are rather difficult to handle because of their sensitivity. Two of the best known brands are Brovira and PMC. Usually to get the best results from these papers we require a negative which is slightly on the dense side and fairly brilliant. Also, quite contrary to the usual directions given, you will find that it will be better to give a short exposure and a fairly long development—at least 2 minutes and preferably 3 minutes—not the often quoted 45 seconds which leads so many amateurs into trouble.

Next are the chloro-bromide papers which are the most commonly used papers today in the photographic world. As the term denotes, they are somewhat of a compromise between the fast bromide papers and the slower chloride papers. The chloro-bromides have good speed so that the exposure does not take too long, although they are not as sensitive as the bromides, nor is their color as blue-black or as cold as the bromide papers. This is because of the mixture of chloride with the bromide. They therefore give medium to fairly fast speed with a bit warmer tone. Of course, among the chloro-bromides we have a great variety of papers, their characteristics as to speed, and whether they give a cold or a warm tone, depending upon the balance between the chloride and bromide characteristics.

For example, Kodabromide is a very fast chloro-bromide paper giving a cold tone, whereas Opal is a slow chloro-bromide paper giving a warm tone, the Opal paper being approximately 6 times slower in sensitivity than the Kodabromide paper—of course all this referring to the normal grades.

The chloride papers are the slowest papers available and in the old days used to be called gas-light papers. They are rarely used for enlarging but are more commonly employed for contact printing; such papers as Convira, Apex, Azo and Velox are typical. We know any fast bromide paper or any slow chloride paper can be used either for contact printing or enlarging if we are willing to adapt the light to suit. For example, if you wish to make a contact print with a fast bromide paper, all you have to do is to see to it that the printing light is so weak that the correct exposure can be given for 2 or 3 minute development time. On the other hand, a slow chloride paper is sometimes utilized in enlarging where we have a negative so thin and so weak that it is almost impossible to give it the correct printing time on a bromide paper. Among chloride papers one foreign make, Tuma Gas, was superb.

FITTING NEGATIVE TO PAPER

In a sense the three different types of papers in themselves can also make a difference as to the type of negative which you require to get best results. For example, the bromide paper should have a fairly dense, brilliant negative—fairly dense so that the speed will be controllable. A chloro-bromide paper of the fast type requires a negative less dense but fairly brilliant, whereas a chloro-bromide paper of the slower type requires a slightly thinner negative but somewhat more brilliant. The reason the latter requires a thinner negative is its lack of speed which can make the exposure times in the enlarger quite often run into irritating minutes if the negative is a bit too dense. While these slower chloro-bromides are among the most favored papers for professional and amateur use, they require fairly strong and brilliant negatives in order to get the best out of them. While speaking about papers, we could roughly classify papers such as Brovira, PMC, Velour Black, Kodabromide, within the fast enlarging paper classification giving cold black tones, and requiring negatives of a dense, normal type of brilliance. The other papers such as Opal, Kodalure, Veltura, Indiatone, etc., would come within the slow enlarging type of paper, giving warm to very warm tones and

19

requiring thinner but more brilliant, or contrasty, negatives to get the best results. Any future changes in manufacturing procedures may, of course, alter the classification of the papers named.

The next item which we have to consider in getting the so-called perfect negative for our needs is the *brand* of paper which we are using. This too, is a variable factor as paper characteristics may change from year to year or often from month to month. When you are a fair to middlin' beginner, it might be a good idea to stick to one brand of paper for a while until you get thoroughly familiar with all its vagaries and characteristics. The thing to remember is that a normal grade of paper from one manufacturer may not necessarily be the same as a normal grade of paper from another concern, which means that if a certain pet negative of yours prints well on No. 2 paper of such and such a make, it may not necessarily print exactly the same on No. 2 paper of another make.

For example, just using two well known makes of paper, Velour Black and Kodabromide: while on the face of it they seem to be of the same characteristics, in actual practice they give diverging results. A negative which will make a perfect print on Kodabromide No. 2 will, when printed on Velour Black No. 2, turn out a print which is too contrasty and this will be true of all the grades in that particular type of paper. In general we can say that the Velour Black papers are more contrasty than the Kodabromide variety. Now, of course, that does not mean that one particular paper is better than the other, it simply means that it's very wise to standardize your negatives so that they will fit one particular brand, otherwise you will never be able to work out a definite system. As a general statement it might be safe to say that Defender Velour Black papers require a slightly softer (less brilliant) negative than Eastman papers.

Assuming that the right exposure has been made originally, then the right kind of negative for any paper can be secured by a slight change in negative developing time.

CHAPTER IV

THE PAPER DEVELOPER

T HE next thing which influences the type of negative which you
use but perhaps not to the same extent as the factors mentioned
in foregoing chapters, is the paper developer which you utilize
in your work. For example, every manufacturer has worked out a
formula which is presumed to be most suitable for his particular
brand of paper. To help to make this clear, let us take the Kodabromide and Velour Black brands. The developer recommended for
the Kodabromide papers is usually D-72, that for the Velour Black
paper is 55-D. To the average worker, developers in themselves are
no mysteries but we like to make them so because then there is more
fun about the thing. But when you take a serious look at the formulas
of 55-D and D-72, you are immediately struck by the fact that D-72
is more contrasty, more peppy, than the other. D-72, for example,
has a lot more hydroquinone and sodium carbonate, chemicals which
definitely make a developer more contrasty if they are present in
large quantities. This might explain to some extent why D-72 will
work better with the Kodabromide papers and why 55-D will work
better with the Velour Black papers. If the Kodabromide papers are
a bit softer in contrast than the Velour Black, but you counter that
by using a more contrasty developer, the Kodabromide paper contrast
will be stepped up. If, on the other hand, the Velour Black papers
are slightly more brilliant than the Kodabromide papers, but you
temper them by using a softer developer such as 55-D, there are very
good chances that in the final analysis you may get a normal result
with both papers. You can now see the good reason why every manufacturer is anxious to have you use the developer recommended for
his particular brand of paper. The photographer, therefore, has his

choice of either sticking entirely to one brand of paper and using the recommended developer, or if he wants to wander a bit and use other papers he should make up the right developer to get the best results. While basically, and this is especially true in the case of the beginner, one should stick to a pet brand of paper, in the long run there are many cases where to get different and specific effects we wish to resort to many brands and many types of papers.

From this and the preceding chapters it should be quite clear to you that there are four distinctive and quite often neglected factors which determine the qualities of the *right* negative for your own immediate needs : First the type of enlarger which you use, second the type of paper, third the brand of paper, and fourth the developer. Any one of these factors, properly exaggerated, can make the difference of one grade of paper in contrast.

ALTERING STANDARD DEVELOPERS

I fully realize the proprietary and stubborn interest most of us have in a particular developer, and therefore, assuming that you now have a pet paper developer which has given you fairly good results, you are probably a bit averse to changing to some new-fangled developer. Despite this, I would at least suggest that two extra bottles be present in every darkroom. Regardless of any present ideas you may have, in order to add further to the flexibility of your present formula, you should have available a bottle of sodium carbonate solution and a bottle of 10% potassium bromide.

BROMIDE AND ITS ACTION

From time immemorial we have known the addition of potassium bromide to a paper developer will do the following things : First, it will tend to prevent fog. Second, it will slow down the printing speed of excessively fast papers. Third, it will give clearer highlights —this means it will extend the contrast and range of gradations in the paper. Fourth, it will, if development is not prolonged, tend to produce brownish or sometimes olive-brown tones.

Even if you have been in photography only a very short time you will have heard the expression that "It is always a good idea to add a little extra bromide to the paper developer." I cannot agree one hundred percent with such a statement. Unless you wish to achieve some of the effects listed above, you may be better off going easy on the use of "extra" bromide. For example, suppose you are used to developing a certain paper to a given developing time, such as 2 minutes. If you add quite a bit of extra bromide and you maintain your 2 minute developing period, it is very possible that at the end of the 2 minute period you will have a print which is not a real black but has either a brownish, olive-brown, or olive-green cast. In other words, if you add only bromide to a developer, you may find it more advantageous to prolong your developing time a minute or two extra so that the tones in the print will have a chance to return to blacks, if that is what you desire. Of course the addition of bromide may make necessary an increase in your exposure time to three or four times longer than normal. This may or may not prove to be beneficial, as it can be a great nuisance if the exposures run beyond a 2 or 3 minute period.

Usually the addition of bromide is recommended with papers having a tendency to fog under fairly long developing times, or those which are a bit extra sensitive and therefore somewhat difficult to handle. If the latter is true, I think a better solution would be to make negatives which are a little bit denser for use with these fast papers. Then it will not be necessary to arbitrarily slow down their printing speed by adding the extra bromide. In this way you will be able to maintain rich natural blacks rather than getting a questionable olive-black tone.

I personally find that the greatest benefit of the 10% solution is in keeping the whites or the highlights clearer in the print and thereby, giving a bit of extra contrast.

USING THE BROMIDE SOLUTION

Therefore, a solution of 10% bromide should be a part of your darkroom equipment, but the next time you use it be sure that you really need it. A 10% solution of bromide is made up by weighing out 1 ounce of potassium bromide and then adding sufficient water so that both chemical and water make up 10 ounces by volume. However, if you are in a hurry simply take 1 ounce of the bromide and dissolve it into 10 ounces of water in the ordinary manner and you will never be able to tell the difference. When you are using this solution, every time you measure out one ounce of the liquid you will have approximately 44 grains of bromide, inasmuch as you will be taking 1/10 of the original ounce of bromide, which, of course, consists of 437½ grains. By having your bromide in a 10% solution you can, therefore, quickly and efficiently add any number of grains of potassium bromide to your developer without having to resort to scales for weighing purposes. One-half ounce of 10% solution would be the equivalent of approximately 22 grains of bromide, ¼ ounce to 11 grains, etc. When you are adding bromide to a working solution in a tray, for every 32 ounces of ready-made solution you may as well start by adding at least ½ ounce or one ounce of the 10% solution to see any really noticeable difference in the results. Of course, you can add more and more bromide to get greater changes, but paradoxical as it may seem, while bromide in itself prevents fog, you will finally reach a limit which, if exceeded, will actually bring on fog in the paper. Although, as stated above, excess potassium bromide will bring on fog, under normal conditions it can be very helpful.

RECLAIMING FOGGED PAPERS

Another useful purpose for potassium bromide is in the case of out-dated and possibly fogged papers. These can sometimes be salvaged by first immersing them for a minute or so, after exposure but before actual development, in a 10% solution of bromide and then putting them into the regular developer. Another, and sometimes a simpler method of salvaging old paper is to add the bromide directly to the developer and then give sufficient exposure during enlarging so that the total developing time for the paper will not exceed 45 seconds to one minute, or possibly a minute and a half. Many times paper which would show decided fogging if developed for 2 minutes or more may be perfectly clear and satisfactory if the developing time is kept down to a minimum.

A third manner in which to save old paper is by adding a certain amount of benzotriazole directly to the developer. This chemical, which is obtainable from the Eastman Kodak Co., is a powerful defogging agent and will, in most cases, salvage papers that are out-dated 2 to 3 years and even more. This chemical usually is obtainable in a 0.2% solution and when first making use of it, start by adding ½ ounce of the solution to every 32 ounces of ready-made developer in the tray. If a half ounce does not turn the trick, add another half ounce, and keep on adding half ounces and making tests until finally you get a clear paper without any signs of fog. Here, too, as in the case of all old paper, it is always advisable to shorten your complete developing time to 45 seconds, a minute, or a minute and a half, and not any longer.

SODIUM CARBONATE

While most workers have been sold the idea that the addition of extra bromide to a paper developer is beneficial, very few of them seem to have paid attention to the great benefits which can be derived from the help of extra sodium carbonate. Quite often the amount of sodium carbonate in any given developer will be the determining factor as to its contrast or developing speed.

I usually make up an extra bottle of sodium carbonate by mixing 2 ounces of the sodium carbonate to 32 ounces of water and adding anywhere from 3 to 6, and sometimes up to 8 ounces of this solution to the ready-made developer in the tray. If you desire, you can double the strength of the carbonate solution by mixing 4 ounces of the carbonate to 32 ounces of water, but, of course, the carbonate will not keep as well when the liquid level falls in bottles.

The addition of extra carbonate to a developer will do the following things:

First, it will pep up the developer to the extent that, from the practical viewpoint, it will seem to speed up slow papers 30% to 50%.

Second, if you have been using your developer for a few hours or for a few days and it seems to have become sluggish, brown, and ready for the discard, the addition of a few ounces of sodium carbonate will quite often re-energize it sufficiently for another few hours or even days' usage. The sodium carbonate seems to act as a shot in the arm and is one of the greatest "pepper uppers" in the chemical end of photography.

Third, sodium carbonate will give you much stronger and richer blacks in your printing papers, so in a sense carbonate can control the final "color" of your print and is extremely beneficial in counteracting the olive brown tone in case you have added too much bromide. Its effects are opposite to those of potassium bromide. The bromide gives you clearer highlights but it quite often harms your blacks. The carbonate will give you colder blacks and, if anything, might have a tendency to slightly fog your highlights, but this only if used to excess.

I more frequently add extra carbonate to my paper developer than I do extra bromide, but in many cases I may resort to the addition of both of these chemicals to the ready-made developer—for example, by adding an ounce of 10% bromide to 32 ounces of ready-made developer I will tend to slow up the emulsion speed of my paper, prevent fog, and keep the highlights clearer. By adding 3 or 4 ounces of the sodium carbonate I will speed up the effective emulsion speed of my paper, pick up extra contrast, and make for richer, stronger blacks. The two of them together can do a perfect job, whereas quite often one of them used alone may fail to achieve the wanted results.

But, to sum up, if I had my choice of using only one of these chemicals in the darkroom I certainly would choose the extra bottle of carbonate because even if its only function were to resuscitate a seemingly old and used developer, that in itself would be worth everything I might expect of it.

When it comes to varying the contrast of papers through the manipulation of the developer itself, you will find that the most effective results can be obtained easily on chloro-bromide papers and especially the faster types. Slow chloro-bromide papers are not as quickly influenced in their contrast by the make-up of the developer itself, although they are very much affected in their tone qualities, that is, in their final colors. In practically all cases, the addition of extra carbonate will give a colder tone to any of the papers and will speed up their effective sensitivity even though in itself it may not have caused any change in the actual contrast. But so far as the average beholder is concerned, even this change may give it the *appearance* of having secured more contrast, and that in itself may be sufficient.

While it is extremely difficult to change the contrast of a paper by merely changing the developer, even if we use all the tricks possible with a developer, such as changing the quantities of metol, hydroquinone, carbonate, and bromide, the most we will be able to achieve, and then not even with all papers, will be the equivalent of one grade of higher contrast such as making a No. 2 paper work as a No. 3.

However, this ability to change even that much contrast in a grade of paper usually means the difference between a good and a bad print and is certainly very important. At the present time I do not intend to go into thorough detail of the make-up of the average developer, because I assume you have already run across this in many textbooks, I do wish to remind you of the fact that a great proportion of metol will make for a softer grade print, while a larger amount of hydroquinone will make for a more contrasty print.

Before we leave the subject of carbonate, it might be well to add a word of caution. If you intend to blue tone a print, do not add too much carbonate solution to the developer for it will make it difficult to secure a brilliant blue in the gold chloride toner.

CHAPTER V

MORE ABOUT DEVELOPERS

FOR those who like strictly cold, blue-black tones, one of the best all-around developers to use is Amidol, its disadvantage being that the solution preferably should be made up fresh for each working day. Amidol is a great favorite with many of the "modern school" of workers who often do not care for warm black or brownish tones in their prints. The greatest success, of course, will be achieved when it is used with bromide papers or the very fast chloro-bromide papers. There is not much sense in using this developer on the slower chloro-bromide papers or the papers with a buff stock, as you are then merely mixing up two *basically* opposite materials.

Those who relish warm black tones or even browner colors by *direct* development, had better resort to such developing agents as Adurol (which on the American market is usually sold under such trade names as Chlornol, Chlorquinone, or some similar sounding term), Glycin, Pyrocatechin, or even straight Hydroquinone.

As a general rule, any of the slow working developing agents will have a tendency to give warmer colors in the print, while the faster working developing agents such as Amidol and Metol will lean toward the colder tones. Again, let me remind you that when we speak of cold tones we mean colors which lean toward the bluish-black and when we speak of warmer tones we mean those which lean towards the brown or red part of the spectrum.

While Glycin, Adurol, and Hydroquinone in suitable formulas can be used on practically any type of printing paper, here, too, com-

28

mon sense will suggest that we should use them only on papers which would in themselves have a tendency to give warm tones. Use these slow working developers on the slow chloro-bromide papers such as Kodalure, Opal, Indiatone, Veltura, and papers of similar characteristics instead of on the fast emulsions.

By selecting the proper developer for these warmer tone papers, you can get some of the marvelous warm black or warm brown tones without any further need for toning. For those who are interested in these warm tone developers, we give some of the best combinations in the back of the book. But if the print should require further toning, you will find that these particular papers, especially after using one of the slower developing agents, will tone very readily. (*See Brown Toners,* pages 238 and 247.)

(*See Brown Toners,* pages 238 and 247.)

USING OLD DEVELOPER FOR WARM TONES

One of the tricks often used by exhibitors who like to get warmer tones in their prints, especially on the slower chloro-bromide papers, is to use partly old, more or less oxidized developer, mixed with a fresh developer. For example, you may have been using a standard MQ developer which after a certain number of hours becomes sluggish and brownish. Instead of throwing this developer away, bottle it and keep it, and the next time you want to get a warm tone result without having to tone the print, simply take this old developer and mix it in proportions of say 50-50 with new fresh developer. You then may get some of the finest brown tones that you have ever achieved. Of course the actual percentage proportions of old and fresh developer should be determined with a little bit of experimentation. You can have lots of fun doing this, but don't forget that many of the most serious workers in the country use this particular trick for getting those rich bronze tones. The trick of using partly old and partly new developer is especially effective if the old developer happens to be one of the Adurol or Glycin type which can be either mixed with a standard Metol-Hydroquinone formula, or fresh developer of its own kind.

STANDARD TWO MINUTE DEVELOPMENT

Before going farther I would like to urge you to develop your pictures for a total time of two minutes. Naturally, I am not going to contend that I personally develop every print for exactly 120 seconds, but I would beseech you to definitely adopt the two minute system if you wish to get somewhere quickly in the printing game.

This two minute developing time is divided into one minute and 45 seconds of actual development in the tray, with the paper completely submerged, and the balance of 15 seconds is taken up by holding the paper by one corner and letting it drain. Do not be afraid of letting the paper drain outside the tray for 15 seconds, but make sure that the emulsion side does not face the safe light. While some technicians may worry about the creation of aerial fog because the paper is exposed to the air for 15 seconds, I have never yet run into any difficulty in that connection. When working with large size papers, the 15 second drain will save you literally ounces of developer during one evening's work and will enable the stop bath to function more efficiently over a longer period of time.

When you start your development, be sure to slide the paper into the developing tray so that it is immediately covered, face up; keep it submerged for the one minute and 45 seconds. Rock the tray constantly in order to insure even development, and it is advisable to rock the tray alternately from east to west and north to south.

The reason I selected two minutes as the standard of developing time is to reach a happy compromise. You will find most good print makers develop normally at least two minutes, and in fact, a great many of them may let their pictures remain in the developer for three and even for four minutes total time.

A longer developing time may give you prints with a richer gradation and of general all around better quality. But, if the safe light in your darkroom has not been properly tested, a three or four minute developing time can give you consistently slightly dull prints without your ever suspecting the real trouble. This same safe light might be quite suitable if the developing time had been limited to two minutes or even less. However, the main reason why two minutes was selected was, of course, not due to either a good or faulty safe light, but primarily because on the average it will give you the best all around results.

I would rarely recommend the short developing times so often used by real beginners or by photo finishing houses who have to work under great stress and rush of time. In many cases these developing times, as short as 45 seconds, lead to all sorts of stains and uneven streaks, and as a general procedure the time is too short, either to get the best out of the print or allow suitable time for methodical work.

Yet, I myself at times do resort to the use of the three or four minute procedure, or in extreme cases even the 45 second "rush hour" system. For example, if I have a negative which might be slightly weak as to contrast, I will make a test strip and develop for three or even four minutes total time so that I will gain a bit extra contrast. In other words, everything being equal, with many papers you will find that by cutting down the exposure in the enlarger and prolonging the development in the tray you will gain extra contrast. How much extra contrast you will obtain will be determined by the characteristics of different papers. Of course, extension of developing time can be further helped by alteration of the make-up of the developer itself.

On the other hand if I find I have a negative which is a bit too contrasty for the particular paper on hand, I may make a test strip and develop only for a minute and 30 seconds, perhaps even only one minute and in some drastic cases may actually leave the print in the developer for the short time of 45 seconds. By over-exposing the print in the enlarger and by under-developing in the tray, quite a noticeable change in contrast can be made in the final picture. When developing for as short a time as 45 seconds be sure to keep the print agitated vigorously the entire time to avoid streaks.

This is all very similar to the same procedure in negative development. The longer we develop a negative, the more contrasty it becomes, while shortened development will flatten out contrast. Naturally, papers are not so adaptable to this manipulation as negative material, but much can be done in this direction. Not only will there be change in contrast by changing developing time, but there will be in most cases a noticeable alteration in the tone or color of the print. An over-exposure with short development will make the print much warmer in tone, and you will get more of a brownish or even reddish color which may be very successful in the making of a portrait or landscape. A shortened exposure with a prolonged development will make for a colder tone, that is, the print will become a stronger black tending toward the bluish part of the spectrum.

31

While I perhaps develop 85% of all my prints for a definite standardized two minutes as explained previously, there are some cases where it is advisable to use either the longer developing or shorter developing times. The trick is, of course, to know when to do it. When you are in doubt stick to the regular method of the two minute time, and you will get into less trouble and get much better results.

Another thing you should get accustomed to is the fact that your prints will always look their very best while they are wet and washing in the tray. Never again will they look as good or will you be as happy about them. The only type of print that comes nearest to keeping its wet appearance is one that has been printed on glossy paper and ferrotyped. All other prints will dry down slightly darker, and, therefore, duller than while they are wet. Some types of papers of the matte and lustrous surfaces dry down discouragingly dull.

If you have any trouble in judging how your prints actually should look while they are wet, you might try the simple expedient of having a print, which looks exactly right when it is dry, placed in a tray of water near the developing tray so that you will be able to compare it with the prints you are making, to better judge their appearance when they are wet. One thing we must keep in mind is that if you are making pictures for professional work or pictures for home deliveries, they should always be made slightly lighter than prints made for salons or exhibitions. The reason exhibition prints should be made darker is that they will be judged or viewed under more efficient or stronger lighting conditions. Prints which dry down too dark can be reduced in Farmer's Reducer (*See Chapter XI*). Their luster can also be improved by applying a varnish or waxing solution over the entire surface after they have been flattened properly. This varnishing or waxing may be done either before or after mounting.

CHAPTER VI

FIXING, WASHING AND DRYING

WHEN it comes to fixing prints, I am of the opinion that most photographers over-fix their prints—that is, they leave them in the hypo too long. In addition they do not move them about sufficiently while they are in the fixer. When you leave your prints in the hypo without moving them occasionally, you are risking spoilage. If they should not happen to be actually flush and parallel on top of one another, any overlapping portions are very apt to be lighter in these spots, where the hypo has had a stronger bleaching action than on the rest of the print. This is true of any of the slow chloro-bromide papers or any of the warm tone papers. Such slow chloro-bromide and warm tone papers should hardly ever be fixed for more than 10 minutes at the utmost and as a matter of fact I personally, when using a paper such as Kodalure, rarely fix it for more than 5 or 6 minutes. In many cases any longer fixing will destroy the color of the print, and more than that, actually lighten up the print by bleaching it.

The faster bromide and chloro-bromide papers are not so susceptible to this bleaching action, but even here I think most photographers make the mistake of leaving their prints in the hypo too long. Do not forget that if your hypo is fresh and in good working condition (and if it isn't in such condition, why are you using it at all?), any print will be quite sufficiently fixed after 2 or 3 minutes time in the hypo to be permanent enough for the next 25 years.

So in the future, when your prints go into the hypo, get into the habit of rocking them for 30 seconds or so, face up, to see that all action has been stopped, then turn them face down and leave them in that position for a couple of minutes. In-between times, as you work on your other pictures, make it a habit to automatically change their position in the hypo bath. If they are slow, warm tone papers, after, at the most, 6 or 7 minutes immersion take them out and wash them. The faster bromide papers should come out after 10 minutes. This is doubly true in the summer time when high temperatures can raise real havoc with your prints in the hypo.

If your hypo is not sufficiently fresh and not in good working condition, even should you leave the print in there for 30 minutes, you might as well know now that it will *never be fixed anyway* and you will merely ruin it. Any hypo that does not fix a print thoroughly in 5 or 6 minutes will never do it in a greater length of time.

Another fact regarding hypo is that in a general sense, an ordinary plain hypo fixes a print much quicker than an acid hardener hypo, and theoretically speaking, a print can practically be fixed in 30 seconds in a plain hypo. A plain hypo bath, however, has the disadvantage of deteriorating much quicker and becoming oxidized through the action of the developer, so that it must be discarded every hour or every 2 hours in order to be safe. One of the reasons why we leave prints longer in an acid hardener hypo is to allow time for the hardener to take action, as the hardening effect takes much longer than the actual fixing.

For many years, the professionals and others who have made up their minds that their prints must last for a hundred years or so, have used two hypo fixing baths. If you have the extra room in your darkroom to employ that system, by all means do so, that is, have one hypo bath in which the print remains for four minutes or less, following which it is transferred to the second bath for another four minutes or less. If both hypo baths are fresh, it will insure the greatest permanency to your prints.

ACID STOP BATH

To prolong the life of the fixing bath and instantly stop the action of the developer, it is advisable to make use of an Acetic acid stop bath between the developing and fixing. This is made by adding one ounce of 28% Acetic acid to 32 ounces of water.

Be sure to renew the bath every hour, or at least every time

34

you no longer notice the vinegar-like odor. There is no sense fooling yourself that a stop bath works all night long, and further, if you do not drain your prints for at least 15 seconds as they leave the developer, your stop bath may be completely neutralized in 10 to 15 minutes' working time.

WASHING

Correct washing is just as important as correct fixing, and many photographers who are extremely careful about using fresh fixing baths do not wash their prints either correctly or sufficiently.

The best way to wash prints is to place them in a fairly shallow tray into which runs a stream of water so that the change of water will be rapid. *A two hours' washing will never be excessive,* although in warm weather 30 minutes may suffice for small, single weight prints. This 2 hour period must be used with large size prints such as 14 x 17's or 16 x 20's.

In addition to the constant change of water, it is necessary that you also change the position of the prints. It is very foolish to merely throw the prints into the tray and then sit down for two hours and read a book. The careful worker will alter the position of the prints every 15 or 20 minutes so each print will get a chance at being thoroughly cleansed with a good stream of water. If you are at all in doubt as to what position your prints should be washed, wash them *face down* so that the emulsion will always be *completely submerged*. Washing prints face up is sometimes very risky unless you make sure to visit the washing tray at regular intervals and keep turning the prints about.

Of course, the best way in which to wash prints is to keep altering their positions and wash them one hour face down and one hour face up. The important fact to remember is that if you have a number of prints which have been washing say, for two hours, and at that time you finish another print, NEVER take this last print out of the hypo and throw it directly with the batch of prints that have been subjected to the two hours' soaking. You then will have contaminated *all* the prints and you must start on a fresh two hour period in order to eliminate the hypo from all the prints. *The time of your final washing should be calculated from the moment that the last print has been removed from the hypo and put in the wash water!*

In many cases, therefore, you will find it convenient to have two washing trays so that if you are working for several hours, it will not be necessary to subject some prints to a three or four hour soaking, which may be somewhat dangerous to the gelatin during hot temperatures in the summer.

The best washing temperature is between 65 and 75 degrees. Below 65 degrees the washing time should be prolonged, and if the temperatures go above 85 degrees, washing is extremely risky and may result in frilling or blisters to the gelatin of the print.

DRYING

After thoroughly washing the print it is necessary to dry it in such a manner that the print will be perfectly flat. There are many ways in which prints can be straightened out, and it seems every photographer has his own pet method.

Perhaps the most efficient way, but definitely not the easiest and one that takes more time, is to let the print dry by either hanging it up by two corners or by allowing it to remain on cheesecloth stretchers. Then when the print has been thoroughly dried, dampen the back of it either with cotton or sponge (of course, keeping away from the emulsion side) and place the print between blotters in an old type hand letterpress. When the wheel of the letterpress has been turned down hard, the print is pressed flat. There is perhaps nothing that will straighten a print better.

Easier and practically just as efficient is to use the regular blotter roll manufactured for this special purpose. When you have a blotter roll with a genuine linen surface, you can eliminate the excess water from the print by wiping or squeegeing as it comes from the washing tray, following which you can place it face down in the blotter roll, fold up the roll and go to bed happily. These rolls come in different sizes, and I always use the very large size for 16 x 20 prints. I have found the blotter roll to be the easiest method of flattening and drying prints perfectly, so when it comes to mounting them they will not buckle in unexpected areas.

CHAPTER VII

THE TEST STRIP AND HOW TO USE IT
Determining The Proper Negative
For Your Equipment

WHETHER a negative is good or perfect can only be decided after we have seen the print. As has been mentioned earlier, what makes a negative good for *you* will depend entirely upon the conditions under which *you* work and the materials which *you* use. Therefore, what anyone else might consider a good negative may be entirely unsuited to your own needs. The perfect or good negative may be compared to the perfect diet for an individual. What one system may thrive on could very easily be wrong for another.

As was explained previously, there are four main points that will decide what type of negative you need. First, the kind of enlarger you use; second, the type of paper; third, the brand of paper and fourth, the developer.

Any one of these factors individually or combined will influence our opinion. Right here we could get very technical and perhaps scare many of our readers away, as it might seem to be too formidable a job to conquer all four of the points. However, whether you are scientifically inclined or not, it is a comparatively simple matter to determine what a normal negative should be for your own working conditions. Here is how I would suggest you begin.

FINDING THE NEGATIVE

Go through your negatives and select three of the best; that is, see that they are sharp and free from defects. The first should approximate your own idea of a perfect negative. Whatever that negative may be, the next should be a little denser or more opaque and *more contrasty*. Your third negative should be thinner and of *less contrast.* All of these negatives should have been made when the sun was shining on a landscape, preferably when the sun was at a 45° angle. At this stage of the game, do not select negatives which either have been taken on too dull a day or under too contrasty lighting conditions. For those who specialize in indoor lighting—whether portraiture, still life, or other type of work—here, too, it is advisable to confine your selection to negatives taken under 45° lighting conditions.

USE NORMAL NEGATIVES

You will easily understand the reason for emphasizing the selection of negatives taken under approximately 45° lighting conditions because they will be the only ones which, under normal developing conditions, will approximate normal contrast. Negatives taken under dull conditions require more than normal developing time in order to increase their contrast to normal and negatives taken under contrasty conditions require less developing time to reduce their contrast to normal. By avoiding these extremes of either flatness or contrast in the initial stages, we will make it simpler for ourselves to acquire the necessary experience and judgment. Second, get a package of enlarging paper of the normal grade, preferably of the size you ordinarily use for your enlargements. We are not interested in the brand of paper you buy. I would suggest, though, that you use a paper of a normal grade of the chloro-bromide type and one having two or more grades of contrast. Third, mix your paper developer and pour it into the tray. I don't care what particular developer you use, although, if you have no particular pet of your own, it is always well to tie to the formula recommended by the paper manufacturer. What we are trying to do is determine the particular type of negative best suited to our own conditions, and the simplest way to do this is make the tests accordingly.

Regardless of theory—and of the fancy test phrases we all pick up—there is only one thing that will show whether we are doing the right thing, and that is the appearance of the print. We are going to make a test strip.

THE TEST STRIP

A test strip is one of the simplest things in photography and yet it is one of the most scientific. As a matter of fact, despite all of the advances in determining exposures and correct printing papers for our conditions, this old-fashioned method of determining what is right for our needs has never been surpassed. At this juncture I do not wish to go into detail in talking about the exposure meters which have been designed for enlarging work. While they are quite useful, they still are not as infallible as a simple test strip. This should be encouraging to the beginner because it gives him the ability to make good pictures without a thorough scientific knowledge of all the fancy phrases used in describing contrast in negatives, scales and papers. But now, let's get to work.

Take the negative which you consider the best and place it in the enlarger.

MASKING NEGATIVES

Be sure not only to mask this negative, but *all* your negatives from now on. What is also important, mask them up to the area which you intend to use in the enlargement. For example, if you are using a 4 x 5 negative and you are only going to select a 2¼ inch square portion from it, you must be sure that you mask it up to that smaller area or you may have stray light reflected from your own clothing or a wall onto the print, which will dull the brilliance. Something that happens very frequently, when we are making large diameter enlargements, is the appearance in the print of "ghosts" or "flares" reflected from bright parts of the enlarger column which will puzzle you no end as to their origin.

Another important point in maintaining brilliance in your prints is to be sure that the lens is kept clean, otherwise your prints will have a dull appearance. You will find that in cellar darkrooms or during the hot humid summer days, a lens can easily take on a veiled surface, and you should make it a habit to check the brilliance of the lens by looking through it when the light is turned on. If you do not want oxidization to set in on the lens, it is necessary that this veil be cleaned off whenever present or after a few years you may find the lens ruined.

Focus the negative mentioned above in the usual manner to the size you wish to make your standard. It is usually best to focus with the lens wide open then stop down to $f8$ or $f11$, or whatever you have determined upon as your normal procedure.

While it is perfectly feasible to use a very small piece of paper to make this test, at the beginning let us be a little more liberal and

Figure 1. Set the clock at zero at start and give the *whole* sheet 5 seconds exposure. Have card ready to move for next exposure.

Figure 2. After lapse of 5 seconds cover one fifth of paper with card and allow another five seconds to pass before moving again.

use one of generous size. If you are anxious to progress quickly, never be afraid of using paper. You will have to waste (if you care to call it that) a certain amount of paper before you acquire sufficient judgment to be on your own, so you may as well start right now. The paper must be held firmly in the easel or frame. Also have available a clock with a large second hand that is easily visible under the safe light and a piece of stiff cardboard. The cardboard must be at least the same size as the enlargement or, preferably, a little larger.

EXPOSING THE TEST STRIP

We are going to expose our strip of paper to the light but not all of it will receive the same exposure. We will, as a matter of fact, give it five different exposures, dividing the paper into fifths. Each fifth will have twice the exposure of the previous one. The total exposure will run up to eighty seconds and will start with five seconds. The intermediate exposures will be 10, 20, and 40 seconds. Now this does not mean that you add five and ten to make fifteen, nor twenty and fifteen to make thirty-five, etc. If you did that, you would find yourself hopelessly involved and it would be impossible to determine the correct exposure. The way in which the counting is done is to give

40

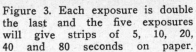

Figure 3. Each exposure is double the last and the five exposures will give strips of 5, 10, 20, 40 and 80 seconds on paper.

Figure 4. After the 80 second exposure has been made the paper is covered and the light turned off. Develop paper normally.

the whole paper an exposure of five seconds, then cover up one-fifth of it and give five more. Move the cardboard over again and give ten seconds more, cover another fifth and add twenty. The final fifth gets an added exposure of forty seconds. Now cover the paper entirely and turn off the enlarger light. Making a test strip is not difficult but at times people have trouble getting off on the right foot. If you remember two things you will find the procedure extremely simple. First, be sure that the entire paper area is exposed for the initial five-second period. Second, no matter what happens, your total exposure must not exceed eighty seconds. If it does, something has gone wrong. When making the test strip be sure that a portion of each exposure covers an area of an important highlight and shadow. Of the two, the highlight portion is the most important as technically speaking we should always make our test strips so the highlight areas come out perfect.

DEVELOPING THE TEST STRIP

You are now ready to develop the test strip. This test strip should be developed for *two minutes* by the clock, as explained in Chapter V. Make two minutes your invariable standard until it be-

Figure 5. A correctly exposed test strip at the end of 2 minutes development. 15 seconds was selected as the best exposure, 10 being too little for the lighter areas of the church and 20 being too long for the cloud and the middle tones of the photograph.

comes automatic. Of course, there will be times when you will deviate from the two minutes, but please not at this stage of the game. The darkroom is one place where one should be a "clock-watcher"; in fact, photography is one profession in which an ardent clock-watcher has the best chances of success.

After the total lapse of two minutes, place the paper in the Acetic acid stop bath and keep it moving for at least ten seconds, then let it drain for ten. Place the paper in the hypo bath and keep it moving for at least twenty seconds, face up, then turn it face down.

Try to make a habit of keeping prints face up in the developer and stop bath, and for the first 20 seconds in the hypo, whenever you are agitating the prints in the trays. But once you leave the print alone it is always safer to leave it face down to insure its being evenly covered by the solution. Both during fixing in the hypo and washing in water, if prints are not turned face down they have a tendency to float upward, so that part of the emulsion will not be covered. This can be very serious later on affecting the permanency of the print or getting good results with toning solutions.

Leave the paper in the hypo

42

 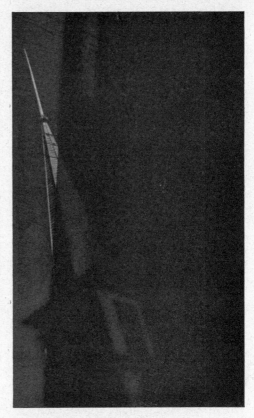

Figure 6. Under-exposed test strip. Either open lens two stops more or, if already fully opened, start next test strip with 80 seconds.

Figure 7. Over-exposed test strip. Reduce lens opening two or three stops, use a weaker bulb in enlarger, or use a rheostat to reduce light.

for ten minutes. Some special papers should not be fixed for more than six minutes and there is certainly no good reason for allowing any paper, regardless of brand or type, to remain in fresh hypo for more than ten minutes. (See Chapter VI). A longer time is almost certain to bleach the print and affect print quality. Ordinarily, at least one hour's washing would follow the fixation, but now, as we are anxious to see how our test made out, we will examine the paper after but one minute in the hypo.

Look at the print under a suitable light, one which is neither too strong nor too weak and will *always* be used as part of your system. (If you examine prints with lights of varying power, it is going to be impossible to acquire good sound judgment, because you can never be exactly sure as to the real appearance of your picture.)

The test strip will show five areas of varying densities, since these have received exposures of 5, 10, 20, 40 and 80 seconds, respectively. You have now to determine which strip was correctly exposed. Most beginners choose an exposure which is too light, but once in a while they tend to the other extreme. There is one test you can employ in making your selection. Study the highlights of the print. For example, if a sky is your important area, determine the exposure by that section; or, if the picture contains a white house and that is the center of interest, the appearance of the house can determine which is the correct exposure. A highlight area usually contains detail and shows texture. If the white house does not show the texture of the materials then it did not get sufficient exposure. Therefore, you should select the next area in the strip—the one that doubled the previous exposure. If all of the test prints are too light, you will have to start all over. Either begin with the eighty-second exposure and double it to, say, 160 and continue on, or perhaps better, open the lens one or two extra stops in order that the exposures may not be too long. Generally speaking, the best average exposure in enlarging is between fifteen and twenty-five seconds. Such an exposure allows for suitable dodging without any great margin of error.

Let us assume that you have examined the test strip and no particular exposure seems to be exactly right—some being too light and others too dark—it will follow that you will therefore be able to pick the comparatively correct exposure by selecting a timing which will fall somewhere in the middle between the two strips which come closest to being correct. Let us further assume you have found a 15 second exposure to be more suitable than either the 10 or 20 second exposures on the test strip.

Place a piece of fresh paper on the easel and give it the selected exposure. Develop two minutes, transfer to the stop bath and finally fix. Now, take your second and third negatives and make similar test strips and prints with them, as you did with the first negative.

When you are through with this work (and I assure you that it will take an entire evening) you are ready to decide what is a suitable negative for your work. No matter how bad your judgment may have been in selecting the three negatives, one of the prints will be superior to the others; especially so if you made sure that your negatives differed as to contrast.

44

In other words, one of the negatives will have made the best print, and that particular negative, no matter what its *visual* appearance may be, is the normal type upon which you should standardize for your work, or at least it will be approximately what you are going to need for your future work, if you desire to come close to a standardized and therefore easier method of making better prints.

If there is still any doubt as to whether the negative is "correct," you can make a further test to determine if it is exactly suited to your paper. Again study your highlights. Have they sufficient detail and texture? Of course, they should have because you selected the correct test strip for the purpose. Now, look at your shadows, that is, the black portions of your print. Are they luminous and do they have a pleasing quality of black, or are they heavy and dense? Are they harsh and completely blocked up? If the separation between your highlight and shadow areas is drastic and sharp or extremely brilliant, your negative is too contrasty for the normal grade of paper and is, therefore, not right. You will need a negative a little softer in quality. If, however, your blacks are grayish and dull and do not have that rich, luminous depth which we require, then the negative is too flat, too thin, and you will have to secure a stronger or more contrasty negative. If something is wrong, look through the rest of your negatives and select one which will approximate the best one you have used, but is either a bit softer or more contrasty. If, however, you find that your highlights contain correct detail and at the same time the shadows are luminous, you should be very happy, for you have finally found just the right negative for your particular set of conditions. This negative should be preserved carefully and its characteristics always kept in mind. From now on, we shall attempt in all our work to make negatives that approximate it as closely as possible. If and when they do, enlarging and photography will be real fun from then on.

In order to acquire judgment so that you can recognize the proper negative for your conditions when you see it, study your "master" negative in a viewing box. This can be an ordinary safelight with the yellow or red slide removed and glass substituted, or it can be a retouching desk. Best of all is to build a special box for the purpose.

Figure 8. A straight print exposed for 15 seconds and developed 2 minutes.

This box should contain a 75 watt blue bulb (although a 60 watt will do) and in place of the slide have a piece of blue X-ray glass. If no X-ray glass is available, use blue opal glass. The bulb should be carefully adjusted so that it provides even illumination over the whole glass, the area of which should measure at least 5 x 7 inches in size; 8 x 10 inches is even better.

If you always use the same viewing arrangement for examination of your negatives you will become an accurate judge of negative quality in very short order. Do not attempt to study a negative by holding it up against a raw light, or one of different intensity, or hold it at a varying distance from the light source. Even a strong, dense and bad negative can be made to appear quite good if viewed with a *strong* light behind it or held close to an ordinary light. Similarly, a thin negative might appear to be of deep density and strong contrast if it is examined before a weak light or if it is held too far from a normal viewing light.

Standardize on a certain strength of light, whether the 75 or 60 watt bulb, and always examine your negatives at the same distance from the lamp. With dry negatives, the simplest way is to always rest them flush *against* the X-ray or blue opal glass. If the box is properly built the slight heat from the bulb will not injure them in the least and by placing them on the glass you will naturally insure the same viewing distance every time.

If the glass in the box is large enough, it might be an excellent idea to frame the "master" negative in one corner of the glass and use it for comparison when analyzing other negatives. If the "master" negative is very valuable, it might be wise to make a duplicate so that no damage will come to the original.

WITH TWO ENLARGERS

In the foregoing I have assumed that you have but one enlarger because if you have a second you may find, to your surprise, that it requires a different type negative to secure comparable results.

If one of the enlargers is of the condenser variety and the other a diffusing type, it will be necessary to make test strips on both of them with the same negative to determine how much their lighting systems vary in contrast.

If they do differ, the *ideal* negative for each one will have to be of a different contrast from the other. This can be adjusted by either longer or shorter development time. (*See Chapter I*).

Another thing which I want to stress is my insistence on the 5, 10, 20, 40, 80 second method of making a test strip. Many of you may feel that under your usual working conditions the times given would be much too long and your print would come out too dark. This may be quite true, but it will happen only if you are making very small prints up to 5 x 7 or such, or even 8 x 10; or it may be due to the fact that your negatives are rather thin and with a strong condensing light the sensitive paper is over-exposed before you have a real chance to make a good print.

In cases where you consistently make small prints, I might suggest that you change to a weaker bulb in the enlarger and that you stop the lens down farther to $f16$ or even $f22$. Of course, stopping the lens down farther might exaggerate your dust problems inasmuch as the dust which may have settled on the condensers may now have been brought into focus by using such a small stop.

Another solution would be to use a rheostat which will enable you to tone down the light output for small size prints. In case you are one of those fellows who likes to work very fast you might even bring your test strip system down to the 2, 4, 8, 16, 32 method, but whatever you do, please always double successive exposures if you wish to stick to a strictly methodical and scientific method. Naturally, if you have been making comparatively small size prints and on fast emulsion, for example making 8 x 10 prints on Kodabromide, you may say that your exposures have been running between 5 and 10 seconds even when the lens is stopped down to $f8$ or $f11$.

Now if you suddenly decide to start making a 14 x 17 print on, for example, Kodalure, you may be amazed to find that your exposures now may run into minutes, and you will definitely become convinced that the 5, 10, 20, 40, 80 method is a very sensible one for average conditions.

In other words if you are working with fast papers and always making small prints, you may wish to modify the system a bit to suit your immediate conditions, but for those who are in the habit of making prints larger than 11 x 14 and on enlargers of doubtful speed, it certainly is going to be best to stick to the longer test strip method.

TEST STRIP FOR UNUSUAL EFFECTS

The test strip method can be used for many other purposes. For example, there may be occasions later on when we will not want to use the so-called correct exposure, i.e., when we are not interested in securing the normal visual effect. There are many times, for example, when a landscape can be made more dramatic by printing it darker than it originally appeared. That is, we may desire to make a deeper print, thereby enhancing the emotional quality of the picture and heightening the drama. Or, exactly the opposite, we may want a light print, that is, a print much lighter than the actual tones of the subject. Whatever we want, it can be determined by our test strip and, in such a case, rather than select the theoretically correct test strip, we pick the one which shows the subject in the manner in which it is to be presented in the final picture. That, too, is a reason why it is a good idea to use a large piece of paper when making the test strip—so that enough of the picture can be shown for adequate study.

CHAPTER VIII

THE TEST STRIP---

Determining the proper contrast grade of paper for the negative

THE test strip can also be used to determine the proper grade of paper for the negative. In the beginning we used a test strip merely to determine whether our negative was suitable for a normal grade of paper. From a practical standpoint and definitely from that of theory, we will always be hopeful of obtaining a normal negative. However, there will be many times when our negative fails to live up to our expectations. Of course, there are methods of correcting such negatives, such as intensification, reduction, or the use of dyes.

In many instances, it may not be desirable to use chemical means or retouching methods, either from lack of time or otherwise. So we resort to the use of a different grade of paper (not a different brand), but a grade of different contrast. You will recall our suggestion that when you choose a brand of paper which you will adopt as your standard you make sure that it is obtainable in two or three grades of contrast—soft, normal, and hard or Nos. 1, 2 and 3. Such a type will prove valuable and flexible in the darkroom, because when your negative fails to meet the standard you have set up you will be able, quite often, to secure almost as good results by employing a different grade of contrast.

To learn how to determine what type of negative is required for a #1 or soft paper—or for a #3 or contrast paper, it may now be a good idea to go back and reexamine the three test strips which were made from your previously selected negatives of varying contrast. Almost without a question, if you previously chose three negatives of different appearance, one of the test prints on the Normal grade of

Figure 9. Determining correct contrast grade of paper. Expose for highlights, develop normally. If middle tones and shadows are *muddy* the paper used is too soft.

Figure 10. If highlights are good but the middle tones and shadows are *harsh* and *hard,* it is an indication that a softer grade of paper must be used with the negative.

paper will have come out quite successfully. But, the second one will appear muddy and gray. It will not have any brilliance; it will be dull. This is an indication that negative and print were not complementary in contrast, and the paper should be changed. A study of the highlights and shadows will solve our problem. If the highlights have the necessary detail but the shadows are grayish, you will have to use a contrast grade paper for that particular negative.

If, on the other hand, the test strip from the third negative shows harsh middle tones, and shadows which are contrasty and black without luminosity, you will have to use a soft grade of paper. We, may, therefore, say we have learned three things in matching negatives to paper.

First, we now understand that a normal negative should be printed on a normal grade of paper; second, that a soft negative is best printed on a contrasty grade; and, finally, that a contrasty negative should be printed on soft paper. A good way to remember this is to think of a see-saw. When one end is low the other is high and at other times the ends are at equal heights. Similarly, when matching paper to negative, use paper of normal contrast for normal negatives and if negatives are of high or low contrasts use their opposites in paper grades.

SORTING NEGATIVES

In professional studios where much work has to be done quickly and efficiently, a well-trained printer or darkroom man will divide his negatives into three piles. This is done with the aid of a viewing light of a strength and intensity with which he is familiar, such as I have suggested for your own use. In one pile he places all of the normal negatives; in a second he lays the flat ones, and in the third go the contrasty. In this manner, after determining the proper exposure for the first normal negative, he can quickly run through the rest of the pile using approximately the same exposure, saving much valuable time. He repeats this procedure with each of the other piles. Of course, in order to do this, he must have acquired correct judgment, but that is something you will eventually be able to duplicate—if you first find out what a good negative is and then use it as a standard. From such a standard it will be easy to determine just how much other negatives deviate and in what direction.

CHAPTER IX

DODGING AND PRINTING - IN

ONE of the interesting sidelights to photography is that it offers a continuous challenge to improve your work. In other words, when you make a picture that you think is pretty good, the chances are, that if you are really progressing in your judgment, you will, within a week or two begin to see that everything is not as perfect as you first thought. This is so even if you have selected the right paper for the negative.

No matter how well you work, somewhere within the negative there are areas which do not quite print out correctly. If everything possible has been done to match negative and paper and the resultant print is still unsatisfactory, we resort to manipulating the light while exposing the print, that is, to either locally "print-in" or "hold back" portions of the image as it is projected.

Holding back and printing-in, in its real sense, is "painting" with light and when done with skill and imagination can change many an ordinary picture into a striking or artistic one. Anyway, you may as well realize that you will rarely get a negative which cannot be improved by darkening some portion or lightening another. While every good photographer tries to make shots which will not require special handling, it is a rare negative which cannot be improved by some kind of treatment.

When you meet a photographer who feels he has a negative which cannot be helped by manipulation in printing you may assume that he is either not aware as to how it could be improved or is ribbing you.

It is rather interesting to note that only amateurs indulge in the little game of arguing the legitimacy of manipulating the light during printing. Never in the professional world is there any question for there we must produce a print which satisfies the customer and to get it we use any method at our command. Without going into the pro and con as to whether darkening or holding back is esthetically sound, I may safely say without contradiction that even our best known purists will use a little manipulation if they feel the print can be improved by such treatment.

MAKING THE CHANGES

In order to indicate what can be done, let us take one example and study the illustrations on pages 55 and 57—the so-called "before and after."

The initial step was the making of a test strip described in Chapter VII and this came out as shown. At first glance it seemed that an exposure of 20 seconds would give us the print desired but after making a full sized print, this proved to be just an ordinary shot. From the 80 second section of the test strip it seemed that the clouds had dramatic possibilities so another print was made, but the highlight areas became too dark and the clouds therefore did not have the emphasis and feeling that we had pictured in our mind's eye. To get the effect we wanted it was necessary that parts of the picture be darkened and others lightened—the obvious method to use was manipulation of the image as it was projected from the lens of the enlarger. After analyzing the two prints (the light one of 20 seconds and the dark one of 80 seconds) a basic exposure of 65 seconds was given with some areas receiving less and others more as shown in the sketch. The final result was the print on page 57. Through holding back and printing-in it now expressed the mood we sought.

The principle of printing-in and holding back is based on the fact that any given area of a print becomes darker when we allow more light to reach it, or, conversely, if we withhold the light the area will appear lighter. This principle is already familiar to us through making the test strips.

PRINTING-IN

Let us first take up the problem of printing-in. There are three principal ways of doing this and the method we choose depends to a great extent upon *what* and *how much* we have to print in or darken.

If a large area must be darkened, such as the outside edges of a picture, it is sometimes possible to use the hand as shown in Figure 16. However, if you find yourself manually awkward, it may be preferable to use a cardboard for the same purpose and with greater ease (Fig. 17). My suggestion is to use the cardboard—your success in printing-in will depend upon your skill in handling it.

Figures 11, 12, 13—A 20 second exposure was selected from the test strip, but this did not bring out the dramatic possibilities of the clouds. An 80 second exposure was then made (Fig. 13) but here the highlight areas became too dark. A basic exposure of 65 seconds was then chosen and some areas held back while others were printed in. See illustration next page. (Figure 14).

Figure 11. The Test Strip

gure 12. The 20 second exposure

Figure 13. The 80 second exposure

Suppose, for instance, that you have a sky to be made darker. Hold the card between the enlarger lens and the paper, close to the lens and turn on the enlarger light. If you have done this correctly no light will reach the paper as yet. This means that you have perfect control over your next move. The amount of extra light to be allowed to reach the cloud section has been determined from an examination of your test strip.

Hold the cardboard sufficiently high so that you can look *under-neath* it and see the outline of your picture when you move the card back and forth. If you should be making a fairly small enlargement, where the lens and paper are closer together, it may be necessary to look *over* the cardboard instead as there would not be enough room to comfortably look under the card.

The cardboard must be kept moving at all times. As a general rule keep it moving from the top of the picture down to where the sky meets the horizon and back to the edge of the picture. In ordinary darkening of corners always start from the edge of the picture, move the card until the light reaches the edge of the area desired then back to the edge of the picture. In this manner you will secure a natural

Figure 14. Following the determination of the basic exposure, the print was examined critically to see what areas should be held back and which should receive more exposure. The result was as shown in the illustration. Those areas marked D were darkened and those marked L, lightened. Note the improvement that has been made over the picture as originally shown in Fig. 12, page 55.

"DANTESQUE"

Figure 15. The finished print with the emphasis on the striking and dramatic cloud formation where it belongs. The alterations were made solely by dodging as shown.

Figure 16   Figure 17

and gradual darkening from the edges of the print to its center.

This simple procedure applied to all four sides will enhance the value of almost any print whether it be a landscape, portrait or a commercial shot. Darkening the sides of your print will automatically and mechanically give you more composition than you will derive out of five books. I am of the opinion that ninety-nine out of a hundred pictures will be improved by this simple method. About the only case in which this may not work out to advantage is in a high-key print but even there it is worth while to try it out.

Under normal conditions we usually desire the center of the picture or center of interest to be the lightest area. By darkening the corners we will, without any trouble, make the eye concentrate or, rather, make the center of interest stand out strongly. This keeps the eye within the picture and prevents it from wandering out or being distracted by light and unwanted areas toward the edges of the print. These areas should be subdued since often their only value is to act as a frame for the important parts of the picture. Either the hand or cardboard can be used for this method of darkening and it is most suitable for large areas.

Of course, we know that there are always exceptions to the rule,

Figure 18

Figure 16. The hand may be used as a dodger by placing it as shown and keeping it in motion during the exposure. The position of the arm must change constantly to avoid a white streak.

Figure 17. An easier and safer method of printing-in edges is to use a card, which should be large enough to cover the print.

Figure 18. Additional exposure inside the print margins can be given by allowing part of image to pass through a hole in the cardboard. Keep dodger moving.

and in some rare instances, it may be more desirable not to move the cardboard too much. That is, not to move it back to the edge of the picture and then down towards the center. This is usually the case when we have a decided, strong, sharp and even outline between highlights and shadows, such as a badly under-exposed foreground and a much over-exposed sky. The cardboard should then be held practically steady but even then it is usually advisable to have a very slight movement back and forth so that the blending edge will be softened. So much for the printing in of large areas and those which are placed around the edges of the picture.

PRINTING-IN CENTRAL AREAS

What about those small lighter areas which are located towards the center of the picture and which make the use of a solid cardboard impossible because then the surrounding areas will go too dark? In other words, what we want now is a method of letting the light strike only the particular area we wish to darken. This is most easily accomplished by having a large cardboard, 8 x 10 or 11 x 14 in size, in which an opening has been cut. You may make this opening fairly large or have several cardboards having different sized openings—in all cases the openings should be placed slightly off center (Fig. 18).

The different sized openings will enable us to print-in almost any size area desired. If there is only one card available, make a fairly large opening and control its size and shape by use of the hand, covering up that portion which you do not require. Another method is to have smaller bits of cardboard, each with a different opening cut out, which can be placed over opening in the large card (Fig. 20). If you wish, you can purchase a gadget made of transparent red material that contains a turntable in which there are cut a dozen or more openings of different sizes and shapes.

These dodgers can further be improved by painting the upper side with white paint, the bottom should remain dark. By slipping a piece of paper under the circle during the painting it will be easy to avoid getting the paint on areas where it is not wanted. With the surface painted white, it is possible to see just what portion of the negative is being projected through the hole. Thus it is possible to bring the dodger down until it is right above the paper surface and increase the accuracy of your work. Such a dodger is shown in Fig. 19.

The principle of dodging smaller or more centrally located areas is basically the same as darkening the larger outside sections—but now we use a cardboard with small openings. That is, we let the light reach only the areas we wish to darken and, what is very important, we keep the dodger moving. Dodging small areas through a small opening is somewhat more difficult and requires a bit more skill. You will have to learn by experience how much the dodger must be moved and how you should manipulate it in order that one area does not become too dark in relation to another.

SPOT DODGING

One easy way in which you can learn to do this is often called "spot dodging." The area is first dodged by moving the card north to south. That is, move the dodger in a vertical direction and when you have gone over the whole area once, then in your next movement, go in a horizontal direction, or east and west. By alternating from vertical to horizontal directions, you may do a very good job from the start. There is one thing you must watch, however, that is, if the spot is a very small one and your opening in the dodger is comparatively large, you may find that the center of the area receives the *total* time of dodging while the outside portions of the spot receive only a *small* part of their quota. The center of the spot will become too dark or "burned up."

60

Figure 19. A dodger with the circle, containing the openings, painted white, enables the image to be seen without the necessity of peering beneath it. This allows extremely accurate dodging for small areas. The underside of the dodger is dark to avoid reflections and fog. The cardboard strips protect the edges of the print when the dodger is brought close to the paper.

This can be avoided by deliberately seeing to it that the central area does not receive more total printing time than any other section.

Occasionally a spot may be very oddly shaped and of a complicated pattern. Such an area can be handled two ways; if it is large on one side and tapers down to a small area on the other then by merely working the dodger up and down, you can, to some extent, control the size and area of light which reaches any portion of the area. When working on the bigger end of the spot, keep the dodger high to take full advantage of the opening. When moving in the direction of the smaller part of the area, bring the dodger closer to the print to diminish the size of the light coming through the hole.

If the area is shaped so that control of the light by raising or lowering the dodger is too difficult, it may be more advisable to do the dodging in sections, using a large opening for the large section then stopping and adjusting the dodger to a smaller opening suitable for the next area. Even a third small opening may be needed in order to complete the job or sometimes the shape of the opening of the dodger has to be changed. You may note from Figure 20 that the

61

dodger might better be made so that it contains oval, circular, and even rectangular and triangular openings. With such an assortment and a bit of practice you should be able to control almost anything in your print which requires dodging or printing-in.

Sometimes when printing-in small areas in the center of a picture, the outside edges of the print may accidentally be exposed to the light because the dodger is not large enough. In most cases this can be avoided by changing the position of the dodger to take advantage of the off-center position of the opening. Where this is awkward or difficult, pieces of cardboard may be laid over the edges of the prints as is shown in Figure 22. In this way a comparatively small dodger may be used on large prints.

DODGING BY HOLDING BACK THE LIGHT

Next, in the printing or "painting" with light, we come to the reverse process—where we wish to make an area lighter. Many times you will find that even in a negative which could be considered normal, some areas print too dark to give an accurate presentation of the scene or the results we want. This fault is quite common in landscapes where the green trees usually print much too dark. The remedy is to withhold the light from those spots during the printing.

This is most easily accomplished by the use of dodgers made of pieces of cotton or cardboard held on a wire (Fig. 23). The wire should be painted a flat, dark color to avoid highlight reflection and

Figure 20. A set of small cards is used to change the shape of the opening instead of using the hand. These are placed over the large hole.

Figure 21. Solid dodgers are made by attaching cards or cotton to a wire, which should be 15 inches long. Cards are edge protectors (Fig. 22).

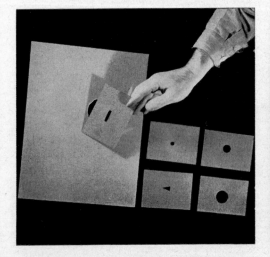

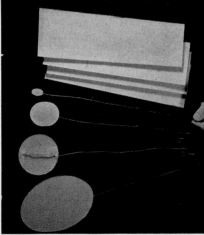

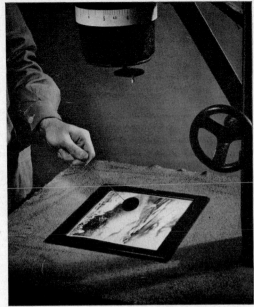

Figure 22. The shape of the opening can be altered by using the
fingers. The cardboards protect the
edges of the print from accidental exposure while dodging.

Figure 23. To lighten an area inside
the margins of the print, a solid
dodger is used. This must be kept
moving at all times to prevent the
appearance of a "hard" edge to area.

be flexible so that it will vibrate a bit on its own account. Also, the
wire should be long, at least 12 inches and preferably 15 inches. While
such a length is not necessary for a small print (up to 8″ x 10″),
when you make the larger sizes you will find the long wire a protec-
tion against inadvertently placing your hand within the picture area
and holding back the light where it should not be interfered with.

These dodgers should be made of different sizes and shapes
(Fig. 21). Usually it is a good idea to make at least a half dozen of
assorted kinds and keep them handy for any type of job. Some may
prefer cotton dodgers, made by attaching a puff of cotton to the
end of a wire. These are excellent for producing soft edges to the
dodged area. One dodger can be made to serve a number of purposes, for the area controlled by it can be varied by moving the dodger
closer to or farther from the paper. For most accurate control the
dodger should be held fairly close to the paper.

The dodger should also be kept moving sufficiently so that no
definite edge will show what you have done, but don't shake it too
vigorously. Some people act as though they were afflicted with St.
Vitus dance when using one.

By continuously lowering and raising the dodger during the exposure further control may be had. This lowering and raising will also have the effect of keeping the center of the area a little lighter by letting more light reach out over the outer edges, which is sometimes desirable.

A skillful printer can, through the use of printing-in and dodging, make such drastic changes in a picture that it becomes hard to believe that the effects were created with the use of these simple methods.

THE BLUEPRINT METHOD

When doing any dodging, printing-in, or flashing on a print, it is always a good idea to plan in advance what you want to do and then *mark it down* so that you will not forget any of the steps. Not only is this a good plan for the work at hand, but the sheet with the various times marked upon it can be used to help make duplicate prints.

Figure 24 shows a typical "Blue Print." The encircled number 20 at the top represents the basic exposure as determined from the test strip. Areas which require less light must be held back *during* the basic exposure and are marked with a minus sign. Spots which require *additional* exposure (printing-in) are marked with a plus sign. The numbers themselves represent seconds of exposure time. If flashing also should be necessary, make a second plan for it underneath the dodging layout. All this is done on an ordinary sheet of note paper or a page from a copy book.

When the print is finished mark such essentials as the lens stop, paper used, developer make-up and time of development, on the lower edge of the sheet. File the plan away with the negative or stock print and then the next time you need to make a print from that negative the "Blue Print" will save you lots of time.

Even if you should use a different paper or developer, the information will be valuable. To bring the "Blue Print" up to the minute, all you have to do is to note any difference between the old "basic" exposure and the new exposure (as determined by test strip). If there is a difference, simply allow the right ratio for all the dodging procedures increasing or decreasing proportionately as necessary and the job will be done.

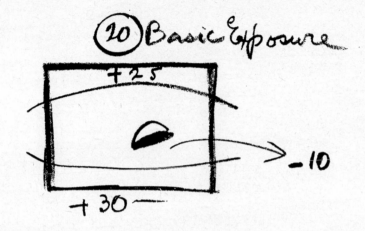

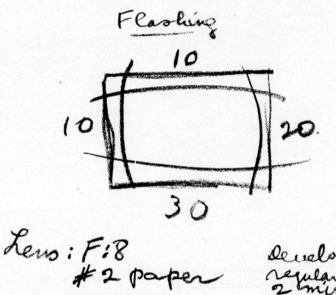

Figure 24. The "Blue Print" method of keeping a record of what must be done to the print during exposure. The areas needing additional exposure are marked by plus signs and those which must be held back during the basic exposure by minus signs. The lower diagram shows the amount and extent of the flashing (see chapter X). After noting the basic exposure, lens opening, etc. on the sheet, it is filed with a stock print of the subject so that later the same picture may be duplicated.

CHAPTER X

FLASHING FOR TONE CONTROL

FLASHING is one of the most effective control methods used in enlarging. Basically, flashing is nothing more or less than deliberately fogging the print, but it is "controlled" fogging. That is, we fog or darken carefully selected areas of the print, the fogging creating its own design and composition independent of the image formed by the negative. Its uses are manifold and once you are fully aware of its plasticity you will be using its possibilities in a hundred different ways.

For example, flashing is a marvelous method for darkening corners and the edges of prints, eliminating distracting areas and adding a greater range of tonal scale to the paper by enriching the blacks. It can entirely remove out-of-focus effects, whether it be the foreground in a landscape or hands in a portrait. A negative with a badly over-exposed, white sky can be flashed in to the desired depth of tone and you will have a yellow, orange or red filter effect without the trouble of attempting to "print in" all this blocked up portion for endless minutes, only to end up with a coarse, grainy firmament. If you have a strong, harsh negative, with very spotty, exaggerated highlights and your available printing paper is too contrasty, you can eliminate the contrast and make the paper a grade or two softer by giving it an "overall" flash. (Figure 25.)

In clever hands, by using cutout masks, new designs can be created and introduced for perfect composition, such as adding soft shadows to flatly-lighted street scenes, or, you can even insert silhouettes of persons or arches to give better aerial perspective.

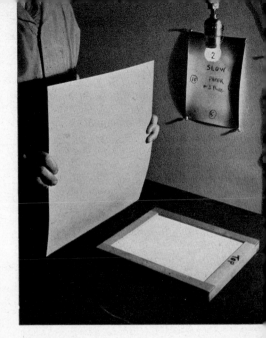

Figure 25. Paper may be made a grade or two softer by giving it an overall flash exposure of 1 or 2 seconds, depending upon the light strength. The same method may also be used to eliminate grain in paper negatives by flashing the paper through the back.

Flashing can also be employed to make simple black borders around pictures instead of using the risky method of inking in with India ink. (Figure 26.) While flashing can, of course, be adapted to any brand or type of paper, it is practically a must with the very slow enlarging papers.

From the foregoing, it is evident that only lack of imagination will prevent us from taking advantage of all the possible applications. In its widest scope, flashing can be as significant a medium to the photographer as the airbrush is to the average commercial artist.

At what particular time during the making of a print do we use flashing? The answer is that it can be used *before, during* or *after* the paper is exposed to the light through the negative. It can be done *before* the print is developed or *during* development. In special cases, you can even interrupt the development completely by placing the paper in the stop bath, washing off the Acetic acid, then doing the flashing, either for the first time or to add to previous flashing. After this the paper is returned to the developing tray. However, until you become fully conversant with all these variations, let me suggest that you do the flashing *after* you have printed the picture but *before* you start development.

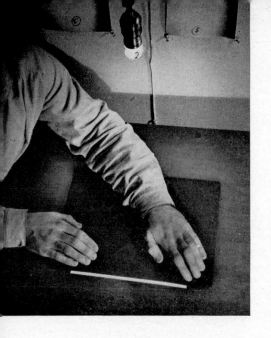

Figure 26. Black borders can be flashed in as shown. If speed is essential, different sized cardboards can be made to fit the standard sized papers. The same setup can be used to introduce silhouettes and shadows in the foregrounds of your prints by using masks.

Next, what fancy equipment do we need to bring forth all these results?—only a light and a piece of cardboard or cloth. Almost any type or form of light will do which gives an even illumination and which can be regulated to give variations of weak light intensities. To avoid "hot spots" an even smooth illumination is naturally a requisite, as in all forms of printing, but the most important factor in flashing is the absolute weakness of the light when it *reaches* the paper surface.

TESTING THE LIGHT SOURCE

An exposure meter can be called into play to help determine the strength of the light by placing the meter on the exact spot where the paper will be flashed. You can check the light by placing a mirror just underneath the meter and using a small flashlight to read the light scale (but don't allow the light from the flashlight to strike the cell of the meter.) If you get a stronger reading than, say .4 (and not 4) on a Weston, it is too powerful for even the slowest chlorobromide papers. Offhand, a light that can be varied to read from .1, for fast papers, to .3 for slow papers should be safe enough.

Therefore, for the light source itself we can actually use a ceiling light, an enlarger, a flashlight or anything that will not be too strong in its fogging action. Our first reaction is to use our enlarger and unquestionably it is the best for the purpose. It has, or should have, even illumination, and it is a simple matter to stop down the lens so that the light will be of the correct weakness for all types of enlarging papers. Despite all these very obvious advantages, I will never recommend the use of an enlarger for this work unless you have TWO of them.

If you have only one enlarger, better rig up a separate system for flashing work; trying to do both the printing of the negative and the flashing all in one machine is enough to drive anyone to straight printing!

Remember that flashing is usually accomplished *without* the presence of the negative itself. If you attempt flashing with the same enlarger used for making the print, you run into difficulties. For instance: with the negative in the enlarger you first print it, then in order to do the flashing you have to *remove* it and adjust the lens to the proper "flashing" strength. Then you replace the negative and readjust the lens if you wish to make a second print. In addition, when using various negatives, you will have different ratios of magnification necessitating also readjustment of the height of the lens from the paper. All these changes offer too much chance for a bad slip somewhere.

Only in one instance is flashing advised with the same enlarger and that is when you are using a flashlight held in the hand to remove small "localized" highlights, at which time you will have the red safe light of the enlarger in place to enable you to accurately direct the light beam. Even then it is very difficult to control the situation satisfactorily. Therefore, assuming that most readers have only one enlarger, I would suggest the use of a permanently placed light in a convenient corner of the darkroom, or wherever the family tolerates your excursions into alchemy.

RIGGING THE FLASHING LIGHT

This light can be controlled by a rheostat or can be placed in a boxlike container, its striking power regulated by a series of home-made Waterhouse stops or the adjustable diaphragm of a discarded lens. Some of the more mechanically minded brethren of our craft will have no difficulty in devising a sound and practical working system of their own. However, for the great majority of enthusiasts I recommend that you begin with the method as illustrated.

Obtain three bulbs of 7½ watts each (Figure 27). Cover up

the first lamp at the lower end with sufficient adhesive tape so that approximately only one-fourth of its light is allowed to come through. Mark this bulb with pen or pencil as No. 1. The second bulb should not be covered up as much but sufficiently, however, so that about one-third of its power remains effective—this should be tagged No. 2. Allow the third bulb to remain uncovered, merely identifying it as No. 3.

Now that they are of different intensities, these bulbs are ready for use in flashing. The No. 1 bulb is intended for use with very fast (extremely sensitive) bromides and the softer grades of chloro-bromide papers. The No. 2 lamp is for the normal and contrast grades of average speed chloro-bromide papers, while No. 3 is for the slower types of chloro-bromides and even contact papers.

Arrange to have an electric socket suspended at least 12 inches away from a wall and a minimum of four feet above the table where

Figure 27. Three small, 7½ watt bulbs; two partially covered with adhesive tape to cut down their light strength. The paper tests show good and poor flashing technique. Note uneven flashing in right hand test sample.

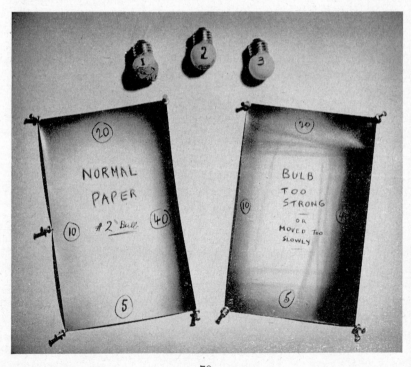

the flashing will take place. You will recall that where an ordinary light is used for contact printing, your light source must be at least twice as far away as the diagonal of the print to obtain even illumination. At four feet, you will not only have even illumination but perfect control over the strength of the light. (*In the examples shown here the light is somewhat nearer the paper but this was desirable for illustration purposes.*)

As you will not know the exact fogging or flashing strength of each of these bulbs when applied to the various types of papers, it will be necessary to make a few tests. But these tests will only have to be made once as they are saved for future reference. Inasmuch as the No. 2 bulb can be considered as "Normal," select that for the first test and put it in the socket.

MAKING THE FLASHING TEST

Take a piece of your favorite brand of medium speed chlorobromide paper, normal grade, and place it in a printing frame or easel. The frame or easel should not have any cumbersome projections along its four sides or there will be trouble from leaking light during the flashing. Write the word "TOP" at one end of the printing frame to avoid confusion later when transporting the frame and paper from the enlarger to the flashing table. For instance, if you intend to darken the left side of a print, you may as well be definite about it and know which side is which. Otherwise, you may be amazed to note after development that in some mysterious manner you inadvertently flashed the wrong side. After all, there are frolicsome Gremlins in the darkrooms too, not to speak of traffic problems.

Next comes another important piece of equipment and that is the opaque object for protecting those areas of our picture which have no business being subjected to a fogging light. So that no uncontrolled light dulls our picture, this opaque object must always remain extremely close to the paper, even right in contact if possible. If you have an easel with jutting knobs or sliding contraptions, then your best bet is to use a focusing cloth or other flexible, non-transparent material (Figure 29).

But, should you possess a smooth-sided frame, then you can use an ordinary mount or cardboard. The minimum safe size of this cardboard is 16 x 20 inches for 8 x 10 prints and 24 x 28 for 11 x 14 and 14 x 17 prints. Or, to put it another way, it should be several inches longer at its narrowest dimension than the diagonal of the print; if not, you may get into trouble when flashing the print in a catercornered position.

Now, we are completely organized to begin our first flashing test. The cardboard (or focusing cloth) is placed over the sensitive paper and the No. 2 light turned on (Figure 30). Keeping the cardboard right close to the paper and not lifting it at any time, slide it back and forth at a good speed, about two or three "slides" per second. Presuming you have started flashing at the top of the paper, you will have moved the cardboard away from this edge toward the center of the print, say, (for practice sake) about two or three inches, and then swiftly back to the top of the frame, again *completely* covering the paper.

MOVING THE CARDBOARD

This up-and-down motion must have variation. First, bring the cardboard down in a straight direction and return it to the top in the same manner. On your second stroke, going down, turn the cardboard sufficiently so that it comes down from the left angularly, returning it to the top in a similar direction. On your third stroke down, bring it from the right angularly, going back to the top in the same fashion.

Figure 28. A giant dodger in contact with paper gives all-around flashing. It must be kept moving slightly.

Figure 29. If your easel has projecting parts, or area to be flashed has an uneven outline, use cloth instead of card.

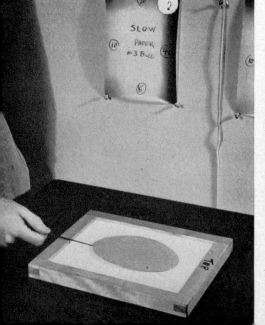

Figure 30. Before the flashing is begun the cardboard should entirely cover the frame and exclude all the light.

Figure 31. This multiple exposure shows the movement of the card during exposure. Note work sketch.

These three strokes, repeated in rapid succession will give a smoothly blended area of graduated darkening, with no straight lines evident anywhere. The reason for the two catercornered strokes is to create a little more darkness on the sides than in the center, something like a small rainbow arc. Of course, if you want an absolutely straight line effect, simply keep going up and down in a straight direction, but this is rarely desired. Figure 31, which was purposely multi-exposed to show the manipulation of these three strokes, should help to make this clear.

If you do not keep the cardboard in continuous motion, or if you do not move it rapidly enough, or if the light is too strong for the paper, you will find nasty black lines or streaks as shown in Figure 27.

Your first flashing should be for five seconds duration. Turn off the light and turn the frame around in a counter-clockwise movement so that the right side of the frame is now in the position previously occupied by the top. The cardboard should again completely cover the frame and print before turning on the light once more.

With the cardboard completely covering frame and print, turn

73

on the light again. You are now ready to make the second exposure test, which should be for 10 seconds and done in exactly the same manner as the first test. After 10 seconds have elapsed, turn off the light and turn the bottom part of the frame in position. This test should be for 20 seconds. Continuing in a counter-clockwise direction, place the left side of the frame in position to complete the final test with 40 seconds flashing.

Following the development procedure as outlined in Chapter V, develop the flashed paper for two minutes, place in a stop-bath and fix in hypo. After a minute in the hypo you can turn on the regular ceiling light of the darkroom and examine the results of the flashing. If everything is right, the five-second test should hardly show any trace of fogging, that is, it should only be very slightly darkened. The 10-second strip should show a bit more darkening and the 20-second and 40-second strips should naturally show correspondingly darker tones but in no instance should any streaks or unevenness be noticeable.

IF THE LIGHT IS TOO STRONG

If your light is so dangerously strong that it can make a marked change in the paper in less than 5 seconds, you are in for plenty of headaches unless you change it. It is an indication that every time you slide the cardboard down to expose the paper, the light is biting into the paper too vigorously and is going to leave distinct marks for each downward stroke. There will be no gradual blending of strokes so necessary for good work.

The remedy is simple—either weaken the light by adding more adhesive tape, or raise it higher. Good and effective flashing should take at least 10, and preferably 20 seconds, before it makes a fair amount of darkening noticeable. Even in cases where you wish to completely darken a side, it is important to use a weak light to do it smoothly, securing the stronger dark tones by prolonged flashing up to 60 seconds or more. If you try to get a quick strong fogging by increasing the intensity of the light itself, you are very likely to run into difficulties and unfairly condemn the method. The one time it might be safe to use a stronger light is in making black borders, or silhouettes, where the cardboard mask is not usually moved.

After making the first test with the No. 2 lamp on your favorite paper, you should test out the other bulbs on the faster and slower

74

papers. These tests are then tacked on the wall near the flashing light —so you will know at all times just how much flashing or darkening you get with each light on each paper (Figure 30). This is a good way of making certain of the right exposure at the start.

Before going any farther this may be an opportune time to explain the difference between "printing-in" and flashing. Please look closely at the flashing test you have just made; all you see on it will be four distinctive shades of darkening or fogging. You don't see anything else. There is no picture there—no texture—no detail, just fogged edges. That is flashing.

Printing-in, means darkening too, but it is darkening which is done by allowing the light of the enlarger to come through the negative itself; this form of dodging will bring out the form and substance of whatever image is in that portion of the negative. Printing-in, therefore, brings out texture and detail. Flashing however, hides it, fogs it, darkens it. Don't try to flash when you really should print-in.

The query naturally arises, if printing-in via the negative darkens too—why flash at all? Well, first, as previously mentioned, flashing will give effects which were never in the negative. But even where they appear similar, such as darkening of corners, the action of flashing is entirely different from darkening the corners by printing-in.

HARMONIZING CONTRASTY AREAS

When printing-in is used, the light coming through the negative is always stronger where it travels through the transparent or weak portions than where it goes through the opaque, strong areas of silver. Therefore, the shadows always come out blacker and the highlights always lighter. This makes it practically impossible to "pull together" contrasty areas which are adjacent to each other. But, when we apply the flashing technique, we expose the paper to a fogging light which hits all areas of the print with equal strength—there are no different intensities to take into account. It darkens both highlights and shadows evenly and equalizes the light action, subduing stubborn highlight areas which could not be controlled by printing-in alone, except at the expense of much time and trouble.

To sum up—printing-in and flashing are two entirely different

75

Figure 32. First step is to make a print containing all the dodging and printing-in, to study flashing needed.

Figure 33. To determine the amount of flashing necessary, the flashing sample sheet is held next to the proof.

methods and have dissimilar effects. Oftentimes they should both be used on the same print, sometimes only one is necessary. Whenever you have an area in a negative which contains actual texture which must be darkened down, it is usually necessary to first print-in to show detail, then the flashing is done on top of this printing-in.

If you do this correctly, you will find the area has a pleasing appearance because underneath your artificial darkening by flashing you will still see the shape and texture of the object. If you don't print in the detail first, it usually looks like honest-to-goodness "fogging." However, should there be no detail or texture to worry about, then go ahead and flash immediately. This is also true if you are planning to completely and absolutely darken a certain section.

If you have adjusted everything so that you have good control over the flashing and you are fully aware of what it will or will not do, you are ready to try out the technique on an actual print.

First and always, make a print by the 5-10-20-40-80 seconds test strip method, select the proper exposure and do all the necessary dodging, printing-in, holding back, etc. (Figure 32). Then study this

76

Figure 34. "LAUGHING EYES." The corners were flashed in, uneven background to left subdued, hair darkened on top, bad right corner eliminated and the intense light on hands and arms toned down to center interest on the face. A cardboard was used to do the flashing, handled as shown in Figure 31.

proof and see if flashing would improve it. Most times it definitely will but sometimes it may harm the picture.

If you decide to go ahead with flashing, you must figure out where the print needs it and how much. This you can do by bringing together the print and flashing test (of the same brand and grade of paper). By holding them as shown in Figure 33 you can ascertain how much flashing is going to be necessary to get the correct shade of darkening.

When you plan how much and where you are going to flash, make a pencil record of it on a piece of paper, jotting down the number of seconds with a rough pencil outline as to where the fogging should be applied. If, upon development, you have made the wrong calculations, merely revise your figures on the paper. Don't try to remember everything without jotting it down or you'll end up in a snarl. This notation can be filed away for future guidance (Figure 31). Also see "Blueprint" method, page 65.

HITTING THE RIGHT SPOTS

Many who try flashing for the first time are a bit worried about hitting the right spots. They wish to know how we can be always sure of hitting the area we want to darken. There are two ways in which you can simplify matters for yourself. The best I can suggest is that you use the print which you have made previously (Figure 32). By keeping this in front of you while you are doing the flashing and turning it in the same direction as the frame and paper on which you are working, you will find no difficulty in confining your flashing to the correct areas. If you do not have a print available you are not starting right because a careful worker will always have a print before him as a guide, on which to base his final calculations.

The other method is to resort to making identifying marks along the side of the frame or a few pencil dots on the print. By making marks on two sides of the frame you can denote a boundary line to indicate how far your cardboard should travel.

Another method by which you can determine where you should flash is to keep the print under the enlarger and have the negative still projecting its image onto the paper—but through the red filter. You will then be able to see the image of your picture in red but, of course, you must then have your flashing light close to the enlarger.

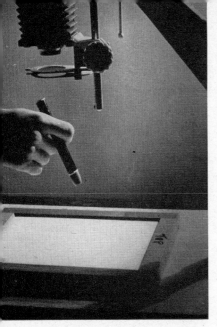

Figure 35. With a red filter in place, a small flashlight may be used to darken areas in the central part of the print. This method is difficult to control.

Figure 36. Flashing may be done during development by means of a small flashlight. Use only when necessary as there is danger of solarization.

Doing the work under the enlarger itself with the red filter in position is best when you wish to eliminate small white spots in the center areas with a flashlight (Figure 35). This could also be attempted while the print is in the developer. There is, however, some danger of solarization if the flashing is done while the print is in the developing tray. (Figure 36). Personally, however, I would recommend that you stick to the method of flashing a print away from the enlarger. The use of a small flashlight for this work sounds intriguing but it is extremely hard to control and difficult to avoid disagreeable and uneven areas. It can be mastered but be ready to waste lots of paper. Try out the three-bulb method first and you will be happier.

How you use flashing, how much of it you use, is entirely up to you. It can be handled so that it is hardly noticeable and in no way apparent, or you can deliberately use it with such abandon and volume that everyone senses something dramatic or drastic has been done to the picture. When and how much you use this method is entirely left to your own discretion, except that in the beginning it might be a good idea to be conservative. If you master it, you have a tremendous extra power at your command.

79

CHAPTER XI

CHEMICAL REDUCTION

C HEMICAL reduction of prints is just as important as negative reduction, if not more so, but many photographers have failed to recognize this to the detriment of their pictures. It is the greatest all-around "after treatment" available and cannot only transform a mediocre print into a prize winner, but add extra brilliance and sparkle to practically any good enlargement. It will take out black spots caused by pinholes, and put catchlights in dull eyes. It will brighten up local areas, put luminosity into shadows, or even introduce new composition by drastically altering tone values. And last, but not least, used overall, it will lighten and pep up a print in the same manner that a snappy cold shower makes us full of vigor and vim.

There are at least a dozen reducers available for this work and although I have tried them all, I am convinced that, all things considered, the best bet is still Howard Farmer's formula of hypo and potassium ferricyanide. This reducer was suggested way back in 1883 for negatives and is still the most popular today, and for good reasons. The ingredients are easy to obtain in any part of the world, it is practically fool-proof from the chemical angle and the results are permanent; but perhaps most important, it is not dangerous to the hands or skin. Reduction can be carried out at almost any time. The print might be several years old and have to be resoaked in water —or the print may be brand new and the reducer applied fifteen minutes after washing, following regular fixing. Also, the action is immediately visible, for when the potassium ferricyanide is applied to the photographic image it oxidizes the silver into silver ferrocyanide.

This is soluble in hypo and the hypo itself is then washed out as usual in running water.

While thousands of formulas have been published covering Farmer's reducer, from the foregoing chemical action it is apparent that the actual make-up is extremely flexible. As the quantity of ferricyanide used determines the real power of the solution, the amount of hypo is immaterial. Most professionals will dissolve a handful of hypo crystals in water and then tint it with ferricyanide to the color of lemonade. The deeper the color the stronger the action and the greater need for careful control. The stronger solution will work very well for the experienced worker but I suggest that you make up the following stock solutions so that you can build up a more methodical procedure.

Stock Solution A

Water	....	*16 oz.*
Hypo	....	*4 oz.*

Stock Solution B

Water	....	*8 oz.*
Potassium ferricyanide	....	*2 oz.*
Potassium bromide	....	*1 oz.*

*The addition of potassium bromide is, of course, unnecessary but it restrains the subtractive action and also prolongs the life of the reducer by 30%.

These two stock solutions will keep at least six months if kept in well-stoppered brown or green bottles. However, when they are poured together ready for use, the mixture is comparatively unstable and may deteriorate within a few minutes or perhaps continue to

Figure 37. The reducer is kept in dark bottles. Blotter, cotton, brush and solution are all that is needed.

work after a half hour. How long it lasts depends upon the strength of the concentration. Usually, the weaker you make the solution the longer it will do the job. You can readily tell when it is exhausted by its loss of color, but in any event it is always wise to renew the mixture every ten minutes.

HOW TO REDUCE THE PRINT

There are three ways in which you can successfully treat a print by reduction:

First—The print must be thoroughly dry. This is unsurpassed for the elimination of black spots and other small areas, or where great accuracy is essential. The reducer is applied with a spotting brush.

Second—The print is soaked and then wiped almost dry. This is the best method for control work on comparatively large areas and is done with a small wad of cotton, or brush.

Third—The print is thoroughly soaked in water for 5 minutes, then completely and evenly immersed in the reducing solution. This is excellent for overall brightening and general contrast.

OVERALL REDUCTION

If it is the first time you ever have attempted to reduce a print, you had better start with the easiest method, and that is No. 3—overall reduction. This will acquaint you with the process so that you may know what to expect when doing the more exacting local work.

Have at least two trays available, one in which to reduce the print, the other for stopping the action with running water. Thorough soaking of the print before starting overall reduction is necessary to ensure even action all over the print. Don't mix the two stock solutions until you are ready to work. The action of Farmer's reducer is a lot more dangerous to prints than to negatives, therefore it is imperative that we start with a very weak solution. Also, it is well to remember that basically Farmer's is a subtractive or contrast reducer. Under normal conditions, it attacks the weakest portions of the silver image first. In a negative, that means the shadows and in a print the highlights. If the reduction on a print is drastic and sudden, the lighter areas may be wiped out completely and the print ruined. However, if Farmer's is greatly diluted,

Figure 38. For overall reduction, a thoroughly soaked print is immersed in a weak solution for 10 seconds or less then placed in running water to stop the reducing action. Repeat until desired tones are obtained.

it assumes the working qualities of a proportional reducer; that is, it weakens the highlights and shadows about equally. To be on the safe side, let us take six ounces of the "A" solution and only a quarter ounce of the "B," *plus 50 ounces of water*. The print having been thoroughly soaked, it is placed quickly and evenly in this solution. Rock the tray back and forth in a brisk manner, keeping the print completely submerged. Watch the clock with an eagle eye and allow the print to remain in the solution for no more than *10 seconds* at the very most; sometimes even five seconds is sufficient. (The softer the emulsion the quicker the action.) Do not try to judge the print now, but immediately jerk it out of the reducer and submerge it in the tray of running water, face down. Wash it thoroughly for a minute or two so that all reducer will be removed and the action stopped. Now take the print out of the water and carefully examine its condition. Is it bright enough? If not, return it to the reducer and repeat the process. But watch the highlight areas, as it is very easy to eliminate all detail and texture. When you are completely satisfied, wash the print for ten minutes and refix in *plain* hypo (such as the 1 to 4 solution in your "A" bottle). Please never use an acid or hardener hypo or I disclaim all responsibility for any trouble you may get into. (The use of plain hypo refers only to clearing after reduction and has no reference to the type of hypo you may have used in the original fixing of the print.) After fixing for ten minutes, wash the print for at least one hour. And that is that.

If a slightly yellow stain is noticeable in the print, it is an indication that perhaps you went too far. You will never get this stain if the reduction is not carried to excess. Usually, though, if you wash the print thoroughly after reduction, then place it in plain hypo, as suggested above, the stain will disappear sufficiently so as not to be noticeable.

If you work in a careful, methodical manner you should never lose a print. A careful worker will often reduce a print in such a manner that the work will take anywhere from ten minutes to two hours.

Should the action be too slow or not brilliant enough, perhaps the reducer has become exhausted and it is time to mix up a new batch from the stock solutions. Or, in some obstinate cases, you will find it advisable to use a stronger combination. For example, if more contrast is desired, you can take six ounces from bottle "A" to which you may add as much as one or two ounces of bottle "B"—plus only 25 ounces of water. But be careful with such a strong solution or "goodbye" print. Remember, the stronger the color of the reducer, the more "cutting" the action. Also, the yellow stain on the print may be more noticeable.

WHEN TO USE STRONG SOLUTION

About the only time you will find the necessity for a stronger solution is when the print has been put through some other chemical process, such as sulphide toning, which has changed the silver compound so that the action of the reducer is somewhat nullified. A print which has been put through selenium will reduce quite readily—in

Figure 39. The local "damp" method. The print is soaked, then wiped dry. The reducer is applied with cotton squeezed almost dry, or with a brush. Apply with an erasing motion for a few seconds then wash off with a stream of water. Excellent for pepping up sky—or even manufacturing clouds, brightening up areas such as snow, backgrounds, etc.

fact, it will become more brownish or reddish when reduced. Reducing in this case should be confined to overall reduction as the color of the print will change locally where the reducer has been applied. Sometimes a print which is too dark and which has been selenium toned and then reduced slightly, will attain a rich brown which will mystify beholders and which is not obtainable in any other manner. A gold-chloride blue-toned print can also be reduced but it usually loses some of its blue, turning toward a green-blue. It is also possible to *first* reduce a print, then do the toning.

LOCAL REDUCTION OF LARGE AREAS

As to local reduction, if it is for fairly large areas (for instance a portion of the sky which should be lightened or the foreground altered), the print should also be thoroughly soaked prior to reduction. When we are ready to begin, the print is placed on a flat surface such as the back of a large tray and completely wiped off with a

Figure 40. Farmer's Reducer is unexcelled for taking out black spots, and lines, putting catchlights in eyes, emphasizing skull structure, etc. Use a strong solution in a small graduate — wipe brush dry on blotter and hold second blotter to check action. Use brush vertically.

sponge or wad of cotton, or in some cases where the gelatin is not too fragile the water can even be eliminated by the gentle use of a squeegee. The reducer is then mixed in a very small tray or a one-ounce graduate. There is no need for the large tray since the print is not going to be submerged. Here, too, it is best to start with a very weak solution of reducer as it is always easy to strengthen it if necessary, but if we start too enthusiastically, irreparable damage can result in one second flat. Have the print almost dry so far as sur-face water is concerned, get a piece of cotton and dip it into the re-ducer. Squeeze it practically dry so that no reducer will accidentally drop onto the print. Place this dampened cotton for two or three seconds on the area which you wish to reduce and keep it moving smoothly like a pencil eraser, but do not try to lighten by actual fric-tion. Let the *chemical* action remove the density. If you rub too hard, nine times out of ten, you will damage the emulsion of the print. If the print does not reduce, rather than rub harder, take a bit more reducer, or, if this does not do the trick, merely strengthen the reducer in the same manner as for overall work. To check the action of the reducer, have in your other hand another bit of cotton or sponge thoroughly soaked with plain water. Place that immediately on the surface on which you have been working and the water will dilute the reducer sufficiently to stop the action. Better still, have at hand a rubber hose with running water so that you can immediately direct a stream of water on the print. The latter method is the best and usually will prevent any difficulty. If you do not have a darkroom which will permit you to splash all this water, you had better go to the bathroom and attach a tube to the faucet there. This type of local reduction is again a form of "painting with light." The careful use of the reducer in local form can make or break a picture and in some cases can actually create something which was not there before. It is a method for emphasizing certain areas, centralizing the interest, brightening up the sky portions, and giving the picture a feeling of form and substance and three-dimensional effect. •

One word of warning: *a picture which has been toned previously will change color in the areas reduced so that they do not match the balance of the print.* Watch out for this. However, a print which is very much in a lower key will take more of this treatment than a print which is in a lighter key. The prints of the lighter-key variety are always the most dangerous to work on as they are easily affected.

SPOT REDUCTION

Now we come to the "spot" method of reduction, where the print is kept absolutely dry. This is most useful for the removal of small pinhole spots or other small areas which have become too dark or which have to be lightened up, such as catchlights in eyes. While some photographers can skillfully remove such small dark areas through the use of a razor blade or knife, usually when the average man tries it he will ruin a good print, either by cutting through the emulsion or at least altering it sufficiently so that the spots are noticeable. This is especially so on some surfaces such as glossy. Even when we try to remove the evidence of the razor-blade work by varnishing the print, quite often the varnish will point out very glaringly the spot treated. Therefore, it is suggested that for all such tiny areas, we should confine ourselves to the chemical reducer which can alter the density without damaging the emulsion. Usually, with reduction in the dry form, we use the reducer absolutely straight. The reason we can use such a strong solution is that by the time the reducer reaches the print, it has been practically eliminated by wiping on a blotter, so that its action is very mild. Perhaps, too, the spot to be removed is usually such a dense, black area (you will remember that Farmer's reducer does not work very vigorously or easily on dark or strong areas of silver) that a vigorous reducer is necessary to penetrate the silver. (Fig. 40).

Now for the correct procedure: Get a good, rounded spotting brush such as a No. 3 Winsor Newton. While some people are very much afraid of stains due to metal coming into contact with the reducer, I have not in actual practice seen any difference between a brush having a metal ferrule or one which is held together with rubber material. Also, have a good supply of blotters handy. Place one piece of blotter on the right side of the print to be reduced; the other blotter is held in the left hand. Make up a small quantity of reducer in an ounce graduate—make it strong, say two drams of "A" to one of "B." To make everything clearly visible use a 75-watt blue bulb in a reflector suspended over the print so that the rays are directed away from the eyes. This enables you to work with fine precision and you can notice every change of density and color in the print. Dip the brush into the reducer and wipe it at least ten times on the blotter to

Figure 41. Shows the print before reduction. In making the finished print, Figure 42, reduction was done in this order. FIRST: Dry print—(1) the whites of the eyes were brightened up. (2) the facial planes were strengthened. (3) the black cord across the chest was eliminated, (see Fig. 43). (4) the gloves were pepped up. (5) the hat received a new pattern. SECOND: print was dampened and wiped dry. (1) the background was introduced with a cotton swab and the chair was emphasized, making the figure stand out. (2) folds of the cape were brought out. THIRD: While wet, the print was given a quick, general, overall reduction to pep it up.

ODFREY EGREMONT, ESQ.   Figure 42

your right, drawing it across, in a turning fashion, to a fine point. Never go over the print without first having almost dried the brush lest you have inadvertent spots which cause damage in a jiffy. Place the brush in a perpendicular or head-on position right on the spot which you wish to take out or lighten. This position, or a ninety-degree angle, gives you great accuracy. After all, you are trying to eliminate a very small spot and you cannot afford to miss or to hit next to it. Sometimes I even use a magnifying glass. If you hold the brush in a slanting position, the chances are you may get into trouble. If the brush has been very carefully wiped, or if the spot is a very dark one, you may not notice any change in the first 15 seconds. Be sure that you do not press the point of the brush so that it flattens out. You are not trying to eliminate the spot by physical force or friction—the chemical must do the work. Furthermore, if you press the brush and flatten the point the chances are that the reducer will spread and give you a big white spot in the wrong place. If you keep your brush finely pointed and dry, any reducer which you deposit on the print cannot spread and will only work on the area where you placed it. If, however, you have been a bit careless and you see the reducer attacking the wrong

Figure 43. The principles of the spot method can be carried farther to remove unwanted details in the print. Here a black cord crossed the shirt (see Figure 41) and this was removed down to the white of the paper base by the reducer. Local spotting then matched the area to the rest of the shirt front.

90

area, immediately stop the action by putting the blotter in your left hand on the spot, thereby picking up all the reducer you have deposited there. A cautious worker, however, will not have to resort too often to the use of this second blotter.

Let us assume that you have correctly used the brush and have deposited but very little ferricyanide on the spot to be removed. Watch it for a few seconds and note its action. If everything goes right and the spot becomes lighter, there will come a time when the action ceases. This is because the small amount of reducer has become exhausted by its action on the silver, and is your cue to take more reducer on the brush, dry it on the blotter, and repeat the application. By doing this very carefully, spots can be removed from the print in such a manner that no further corrective measure with pencil or spotting is necessary. However, if you have carried the action too far and now have a decided white spot where previously there was a black one, this can be taken care of later on with local spotting.

When all black spots have been removed, follow the same procedure as in the overall and local reduction—wash the print for ten minutes, fix in plain hypo, and wash for an hour. Don't ever skip this or the color of the print will change with the lapse of time. This washing, refixing in plain hypo and washing for one hour must be done even for the smallest spot! Don't think that the color will not eventually change, for it will.

If any stain remains in the print after washing and fixing, immerse it in a 5% Sodium bisulphite bath before the final wash. (Sodium sulphite or Potassium metabisulphite will also do.) This may remove all traces of discoloration. However, if yellow or red stains persist, wash the print thoroughly and let dry. Then, bleach it in the Chromium Intensifier (see Chapter XII) and redevelop in ordinary developer. This last treatment will usually eliminate all reducing stains, although the print may become slightly warmer in tone.

Get a few of your old prints and try out all three methods. See how easy it is to clear up the whites of the eyes, introduce highlights in the face itself, make your clouds the brightest ever, or introduce a touch of sunshine in a dull road. Pretty soon, no matter what happens, you will be able to save every dull enlargement—and that really means something!

CHAPTER XII

PRINT INTENSIFICATION

No matter how careful we may be in the exposure and development of our prints, after a day's work there will always be a few which are either too dark or too light. This trouble may not really be apparent until the prints have dried down as all prints give a false indication of their actual appearance while they are still wet. Therefore, the really critical photographer does not give a final appraisal to his work until the following day. Prints which have dried down and seem too muddy can be made brilliant again by the reduction method as described in the previous chapter. But what about pictures which are much too light or which have a weak grayish or brownish tone?

Hundreds of prints, which are thrown away by disappointed photographers because of a deficiency in printing strength, could be saved from the waste basket by the simple process of intensification.

Only recently, a well-known worker in New York photographic circles won a prize with an enlargement which was technically considered beyond hope, until it had been put through the intensification process. Besides the time involved in starting all over again and making new prints, much waste of material can be avoided by resorting to this economical, corrective measure.

The results of intensifying a print are usually two-fold: First, if the print is weak, it will almost invariably show greater density and snap; second, in almost all cases the tonal quality will be greatly improved, the resulting image usually turning out to be a rich warm brown or at least a finer black than was obtained by the original development. How much intensification is secured and how much change of color is obtained depends upon the type of developer used, the strength of the intensifier and very importantly, the kind and type of paper which is being treated, for example Kodalure reacts most satisfactorily.

While the *exact* results cannot be predicted because of all these possible variations, as a general rule you should expect the print to become "warmer" (brownish) in color. Excellent results can be expected with portraits, autumn landscapes, sunsets, or any type of picture which might be enhanced by a warmer tone. Pictures in which cold (bluish) tones should predominate, such as snow scenes, will not react too well, although rather than discard the print I would definitely urge you to put it through the routine first to see what happens. Intensification is also a great help to those who indulge in making paper negatives, as it will often strengthen the paper transparency or the paper negative itself to just the correct contrast for brilliant contact printing on enlarging papers. Anyone who uses lantern slides should also be aware of this easy method for pepping up anemic scenes.

THE INTENSIFIER

Of all the negative intensifiers available, the Chromium Intensifier is about the only one which is suitable for increasing the strength of a print. Mercury salts are not only poisonous but they usually result in a coarse, grainy image with an overall stain in the highlights. Chromium is much safer to use, both as to the comparative non-poisonous make-up of the formula and the relative absence of stains. Only two chemicals are needed, *potassium bichromate* and *hydrochloric acid,* and it is always best to make up the intensifier in two stock solutions which will keep extremely well if kept in brown bottles or stored in the darkroom. A good average formula would be as follows:

Stock Solution A

Water .... 16 oz.
Potassium Bichromate .... 1 oz.

Stock Solution B

Water .... 16 oz.
Hydrochloric Acid C. P. .... 1¾ oz.

Only one caution is necessary when making up these stock solutions. If in doubt about the quality of the available water supply in your locality, use only distilled water and you will have no troubles. However, in most cases ordinary tap water will serve satisfactorily.

While there is still some dispute as to the exact manner in which the chemicals do their work, it is sufficient for the practical worker to know that potassium bichromate is an oxidizer (similar to ferricyanide) and when combined with an amount of weak hydrochloric acid will bleach the print. After sufficient washing the print is redeveloped in any standard paper developer.

To some extent the final result depends on the quantity of hydrochloric acid used. In most instances the more acid used, the less the intensification, but if you use too little, the color of the print may suffer, also the acid is often modified by the presence of calcium carbonate in the water. Until you get better acquainted with the process, I would suggest you start off with one ounce of Stock Solution "A" and one ounce of Stock Solution "B" plus six ounces of water. (Of course, for large sized prints you had better multiply all these amounts four or even eight times, but how much solution you actually need,

Figure 44. This shows the original print before the chrome intensification was applied. Note the lack of detail in the highlights and the general tonal weakness apparent in the picture. Compare this with Figure 45 on next page.

94

I will leave to your own good judgment.) Almost any amount of variation is possible and entirely up to our own discretion but give the above a try before going off on your own.

When you are ready to use this method, first soak the dry print ten minutes in a tray of clean water to insure even action during bleaching. The well-soaked print is then transferred to the bleaching mixture and *continuously* rocked for a minimum of two minutes, or until most of the image has either disappeared or at least become a faded brown. If, at the end of two minutes, the print does not seem to have changed much, continue the bleaching action for another couple of minutes. Should the picture still act in a balky manner after being immersed four or five minutes, it may indicate that you have to strengthen the bleacher. Some prints can be very stubborn, especially if they have been hardened much or have not been thoroughly soaked. Also there will be times during the bleaching when strange and horrifying spots will become visible but don't be too alarmed. Usually, such streaks will respond to the same treatment as a stubborn print: that is, double or triple the strength of the intensifier, such as 8 ounces of "A," two ounces of "B," 6 ounces of water. I have rarely met a print that will not bleach correctly if it is bleached sufficiently long or if the bleacher is strengthened to the bursting point. Sometimes I

Figure 46. Here, a landscape has been subjected to the intensification process with the results shown in Figure 47. A comparison of these two illustrations will show the improvement in tone and drama.

96

WINTER COMES

Figure 47

have bleached a really obnoxious one as long as ten minutes until finally all disturbing marks had disappeared. If, however, despite all your bleaching efforts some stains refuse to vanish, there is still a splendid opportunity that they will go away during re-development.

Let us assume that after two to four minutes bleaching, the print has the correct appearance, which means that it is ready for washing. Washing is extremely important and can determine the success or failure of the treatment. I usually wash bleached prints for at least an hour in running water which has a temperature of about 70 degrees. Anything shorter than that, especially in cold water, may prevent the correct re-development of the image or result in permanent stains. So, please don't use a short-cut on the washing and be sure that every trace of the bichromate is eliminated before the next move. You can easily tell when the print is ready for development by the clear color of the water; the slightest yellow stain in the washing water is a danger sign.

RE-DEVELOPING THE IMAGE

Re-development or blackening of the image can be done with any non-staining paper developer, such as Amidol or Metol-Hydrochinone. Amidol is very fine in some ways especially if there is danger of softening the emulsion too much. You will recall that when an emulsion is first placed into an acid solution (such as the intensifier) and then immersed into an alkali (the carbonate in the Metol-Hydrochinone) that it is being subjected to great stresses with resultant softening and great chance of damage to the gelatin. As Amidol is used without an alkali, this danger is greatly lessened. However, if you should have neglected to wash the print thoroughly, Amidol can give you the finest red stains in your photographic career. Despite this some workers prefer it. The formula is easily mixed:— (*Also see formula page* 246).

Water	*32 oz.*
Amidol	*96 gr.*
Sodium sulphite ....*1¼ oz., 90 gr.*	
Potassium bromide	*8 gr.*

Personally, I usually stick to a standard M-Q developer and watch for signs of frilling. If I suspect that the emulsion may give trouble, I make up a hardener and have it handy so that the print can be placed in it shortly after re-development followed by a few rinses in water. Do not use a hypo hardening fixing bath unless the print has been thoroughly washed previously or else the print will be reduced instead of being intensified.

Inasmuch as I want to make sure that sufficient intensification will take place, I make it a point to use a *fresh,* strong, concentrated developer with a minimum amount of bromide. When the print has been sufficiently washed, slip it into the developer and rock it briskly for at least two minutes, although five minutes is not too much. If everything has been properly carried out, the image should return strong and rich in color. After re-development (no fixing, of course, is necessary) wash the print for one-half hour. When drying, should the emulsion feel a bit soft and slippery to the touch, better hang up the print first and let it completely dry before trying to press it between blotters; you can always resoak it after the emulsion has had a chance to harden or merely wet the back before pressing it flat.

REPEATING THE PROCESS

Should the first attempt at intensification turn out to be a bit of a failure, it is possible to repeat the whole process all over again with a good chance of success. That is, bleach the print, wash and re-develop it. However, it is always best to secure the right results at the first attempt; therefore, if you think the print needs much intensification, start right in with strong solutions both as to intensifier and developer. Of course, a second attempt at intensification will have a real softening effect on the gelatin and should never be attempted until the print has been thoroughly dried first. Also, here it may be advisable to reharden the emulsion, or even to resort to the Amidol developer which would, of course, minimize the tendency of frilling.

In case you are in an awful hurry, it is possible to expedite the removal of the bichromate after bleaching by placing the print in a weak solution of potassium metabisulphite. Another method of shortening the washing period between bleaching and re-development is to immerse the bleached print for 10 to 20 seconds in a 3% solution of sodium carbonate. However, all these "short-cut" methods, while feasible, have some drawbacks to them; if too much metabisulphite is used, the print will come out weaker rather than stronger, and the carbonate increases the danger of frilling. In the beginning stick to straight washing and plenty of it to remove the bichromate.

All this work can be carried out in the usual artificial light available in the darkroom—or even weak daylight. However, do not use too strong a light at any time, especially during re-development or do not allow the print to be exposed *too long* to even a weak light. This is to avoid solarization of the silver chloride—and, of course, stains may be caused through the action of such light, and we have already cautioned about the stains which result from insufficient washing after bleaching.

If you do run into stains, it is quite often possible to eliminate them by re-bleaching the print in an equal amount of potassium bichromate and hydrochloric acid such as one ounce of "A," one ounce of "B," and 6 ounces of water. After bleaching, wash well and re-develop in the usual manner.

My own experience has been that the most beautiful results have been obtained on slow chloro-bromide and chloride papers where the print not only became intensified but picked up a brown tone superior to that produced by the average toning solutions. However, fine work has been done with the faster papers when it may not be desirable to secure too warm tones. While in some cases, intensification is possible

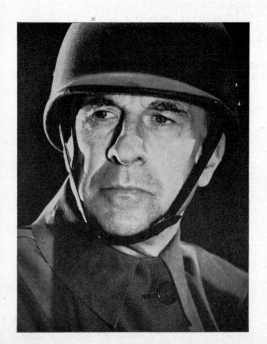

Figure 48. The poor detail in the highlight portions of the face and the general lack of emphasis were corrected by intensifying the print. See illustration on the opposite page.

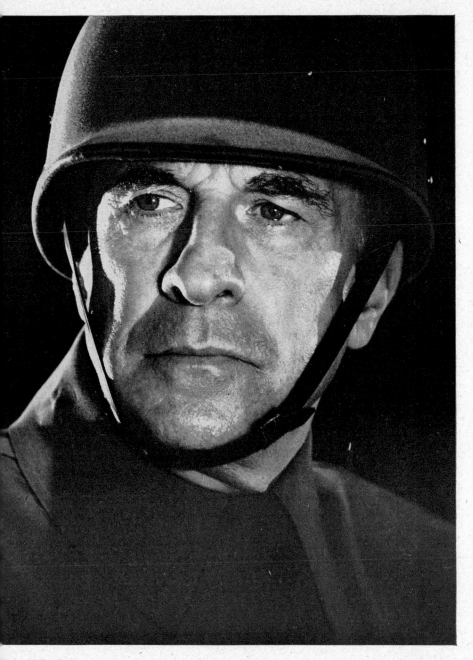

Figure 49

even on prints which have been reduced with Farmer's reducer or toned with "direct" toners such as selenium, it is always best to have a print which has not been previously subjected to other chemical reactions. You can always try "direct" toning afterwards, if necessary. Blue-toned prints are definitely not suitable for this treatment. Also local intensification is not practical because of the change of local color.

CHAPTER XIII

COMBINATION PRINTING

O NE of the most intriguing subjects to the average photographer is the combination of two or more separate negatives into one picture. Many who would like to attempt it are deterred by the thought of technical problems, whereas the real truth of the matter is that if you can make a simple enlargement you can make a combination print. That is, if for your first attempt you choose a simple method, because there are about as many forms and methods of Combination Printing as there are secret developing formulas. Therefore, for our first venture we are going to select an old but efficient and simple method—that of using cut-out cardboard masks to blend the negatives into one harmonious print. When you become manually expert, you can often combine more than two negatives, but let us take it a bit easy and solve a comparatively simple problem: printing in a cloud negative on top of a foreground.

The most difficult thing in this type of combination printing is not mechanical nor technical—rather it is making up our minds which two negatives can be joined together without upsetting Nature's laws or our friends' tempers. However, it is amazing how few people really can pick out a combination print from a straight one—if you don't give them a hint first. I have come across too many who picked an honest-to-goodness straight print as the manipulated one ever to worry again about that part of the problem. Naturally, some common sense must be employed in selecting our material and it seems only logical to try to use two negatives in which the lighting comes from the same direction, or which were taken approximately from the same angle. It is looking for trouble, for example, to combine a cloud

Figure 50. A shot from the file supplies the foreground.

taken while the camera was pointed upward into the sky with a landscape negative where the camera viewpoint is downward.

The best approach to our problem is to start collecting a goodly number of cloud negatives—taken under all sorts of conditions—at all hours of the day and during all seasons. If you are interested in this phase of photography, keep your camera handy, always ready to record interesting cloud formations which come your way. One

Figure 51. The cloud to be combined with above picture.

Figure 52

of my favorite pictures is the result of combining a sunset taken in 1925 with a landscape of the vintage of 1933. Nature does not "date," fortunately, and negatives taken years apart will not show their difference in years.

Assuming that we have selected a half dozen interesting cloud formations and foreground subjects, it would be a fine idea to make a straight enlargement of each, in order to more thoroughly study their possibilities. It is much easier to make final selections by having full-size pictures in front of you—and, as a matter of fact, I usually have dozens of prints filed away for just such a purpose. (See Figs. 50 and 51.)

MATCHING THE NEGATIVES

After having decided which two negatives are going to be joined into one picture, the next step is to determine if the contrast scale of the "selectees" corresponds sufficiently so they will print with snap and vigor on the same piece of enlarging paper. In other words, do not add to your burdens by trying to join a very flat negative with one of great contrast. From a strictly practical point of view, it is not going to matter on what grade of paper they will make the finest print (whether it be #2 or #4), but it is important that both negatives fit on the same grade, or the print quality will suffer accordingly. If the negatives should differ materially as to printing contrast, it will be advisable to use corrective measures in order that they will give a more uniform result. This can often be done by putting one of the negatives either through the intensification or reduction process, according to what the diagnosis calls for. (Reduction or intensification of negatives is basically similar to that of prints, and the same formulas and methods can be used as described in Chapters XI and XII.) If the negatives are so far apart in characteristics that it does not seem feasible to get them to print well on the same sheet of paper, then it is best to resort to the "montage" method of combination, which will be covered in another chapter.

Assuming that in this instance your two negatives are well behaved and do print well on your favorite brand of paper, you are ready to proceed with the actual work.

Before you start, I suggest that you get together the following materials:

106

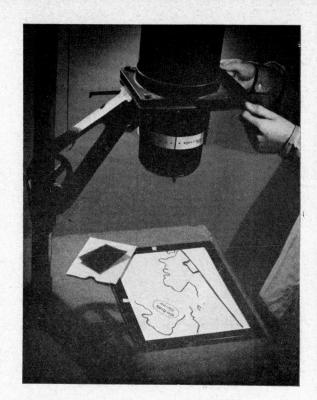

Figure 53. The first pencil preview of the finished picture, made by placing a piece of paper in the easel and lining up both foreground and cloud negatives as they will appear in the finished print. A pencil tracing is made of both for final checkup. The finished picture (Figure 52, page 105) was secured by combining the two negatives as shown in the outline guide. To get the desired result it was necessary to reverse the cloud negative from right to left. Extra printing time was given to the sides and central area of the cloud negative and the foreground negative received double printing time toward the bottom. See chart—Fig. 54.

Enlarging easel or printing frame.

A white piece of paper (on which to outline the composition). This should be the same size and thickness as the enlarging paper which you intend to use, therefore the back of an old print will do. (This is called the Outline Guide.)

An opaque but fairly thin cardboard (to be used for the cutout masks). Should be at least as large as the Outline Guide and preferably somewhat larger.

Two pencils, one "hard," the other "soft," such as Eastman's Negative Pencil.

A pair of scissors or a razor blade.

MAKING THE OUTLINE GUIDE

Take the white sheet of paper (Outline Guide) and place it in the easel or printing frame. Place the negative which will have the greatest influence on the composition in the enlarger first: this is your basic negative and in ninety per cent of landscape arrangements will prove to be the foreground negative. With the enlarging lens wide open, adjust the size of the projected image until it covers the right amount of foreground area on the white sheet of paper. This initial adjustment will usually take a bit of time but don't worry too much about it at this stage of the game. After arriving at the approximate composition, focus the image sharply, but do not as yet stop the lens down. With the hard pencil lightly trace the outline of the horizon or skyline. Don't attempt to make the pencil tracing too definite or permanent as yet, as nine times out of ten it will need some readjustment to either a larger or smaller size, when checked with the cloud negative. After tracing this foreground outline, remove the negative but allow the white sheet of paper to remain in the easel on the enlarging table.

PLACING THE CLOUDS

Now place the cloud negative in the enlarger and with the white sheet as a guide try to fit the composition of the clouds to harmonize with the pencil tracing of the foreground. If you are extremely fortunate, you may find that the cloud negative takes exactly the same height and focusing arrangement as the foreground. But, usually, it will be necessary to readjust the height of the enlarger, so that the second negative will give an agreeable composition. This makes it necessary to re-focus the lens at the new distance from the enlarging easel. Also, by moving the cloud negative around in the carrier (if your enlarger permits this operation) or by shifting the enlarging easel, it will in many cases be possible to find the best place for the clouds in relation to the foreground diagram—or in some cases the solution will be found in completely reversing the negative. Whatever may be necessary should be done, and then lightly trace the most important outlines of the cloud formation on the same sheet of paper on which you traced the foreground. When you turn off the enlarging light you will have your first pencil "preview" of the proposed combination. Look at it critically and see if it needs further checking; usually it does, which means removing the cloud negative and going back to the foreground negative to determine whether a larger or smaller foreground may be more suitable with the present cloud formation. When you are really satisfied with the set-up, take the soft pencil and strongly reinforce the light pencil tracings of both foreground and clouds on the white sheet of paper. This bold and final pencil tracing should be marked "Outline Guide" and must be kept intact for later use in lining up the two negatives on the enlarging paper. (See Fig. 53.)

108

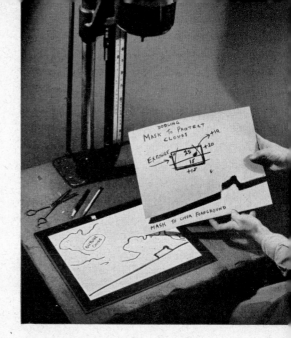

Figure 54. A piece of light card-board is placed over the outline guide (shown in easel) and the foreground negative projected upon it. Any alignment needed can be made by consulting the outline guide. The main picture lines are traced and the card cut apart, one section forming the mask to protect the clouds, while the foreground is printed in and the other becoming a foreground mask to protect the foreground while printing in the clouds. Note the exposure plan drawn on the upper part of the mask. This serves as a guide and shows where additional exposure or less exposure is necessary *during* the printing.

CUTTING THE MASKS

Now that we know the exact size and shape of the combination, we can cut out the masks which will be needed when blending the two negatives during the actual printing. Take an opaque but pliable cardboard and place it over the Outline Guide on the easel. Project the foreground negative and with the hard pencil again trace the skyline, but this time on the cardboard. Turn off the enlarger light and with a sharp scissors, or razor blade, cut the cardboard into two parts, carefully following the pencil outline. On the lower section write "Mask to cover foreground," or some similar identifying mark. (See Fig. 54.) While in the majority of cases it should be possible to identify which mask is for the clouds and which for the foreground, there will be instances where the two sections bear a confusing resemblance to each other. Reaching for the wrong mask in the darkroom at the time of printing will be avoided if they are properly marked at the time of cutting them apart.

DETERMINING CORRECT ENLARGING TIME

In a sense, the most difficult part of the work is now over and we are ready to determine the correct enlarging time for both negatives. After all, using two different negatives, usually at different distances from the easel, it stands to reason it would be extremely un-

109

Figure 55. A pair of test strips, made on one piece of paper, to determine proper printing time for both negatives. The strip can be made on two separate pieces of paper provided both are given the same development.

usual if the enlarging time for both negatives would be identical. First, stop the lens down to a reasonable opening, say ƒ8 or ƒ11, depending on your favorite printing time. Keep the Outline Guide in the enlarging easel. Take a sheet of sensitive paper and cut it in two. By looking at the pencil tracing on the Outline Guide you will see where to place one cut portion of the sensitive paper to make a test strip of the most important portions of the foreground negative. Make the test strip in the correct manner of the 5, 10, 20, 40, 80-second method (as outlined in chapter VII). After making the test strip, do not develop it immediately but place it in some safe place for the time being. Now remove the foreground negative and replace it with the cloud scene. Line up the cloud negative to its proper size by using the pencil composition of the Outline Guide, re-focusing if this is called for. Using the other portion of the sensitized paper, make the usual test strip, but this time for the most important areas of the cloud negative. After this is done, take the two test strips, foreground and cloud, and develop for exactly the same length of time. After development, stop bath, and hypo bath, turn on the white light and examine the two strips carefully to determine the correct printing time for both negatives. If desired, these two tests can be made on the same piece of paper (See Fig. 55).

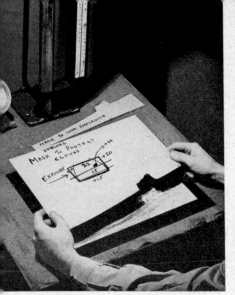
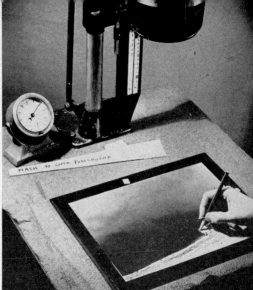

Figure 56. Hold the cloud mask as shown while printing-in the foreground. Allow a certain amount of spill of the foreground negative into the cloud area. The mask should be kept moving during exposure.

Figure 57. For identification, place pencil dots inside first exposure under red filter. These marks should be rubbed off with the finger as soon as paper is in tray for development to avoid white spots on the print.

When you have decided on the correct exposure as shown by the test strips, make the customary exposure-time notations on the cut-out mask. I know that you have a fine memory, but it is always safer to mark things down in black and white—just in case there is a telephone interruption or something to throw you out of gear. These exposure notations should roughly imitate the shape of the proposed combination print with all details marked as to extra seconds for printing-in or holding back (See Fig. 56). When everything is figured out, put the foreground negative back in the enlarger (or whichever negative is the influencing factor in determining the composition). Readjust to the proper height as called for by the Outline Guide, but don't disturb the position of the easel. Take a full-size sheet of enlarging paper and mark one side "Top" on the back of the paper. This will often save time at later stages when attempting to determine quickly which is top or bottom. Place this sensitive paper in the enlarging easel in the same position as previously occupied by the Outline Guide. Take the top portion of the cut-out marked "Mask to protect clouds" and hold it near the paper so as to closely fit the space to be occupied by the clouds. (See Fig. 56.) Turn on the enlarging light and you're off!

In all cases of combination printing the success or failure of the job will be determined by your ability to "blend" the two negatives together. I believe that almost everything goes wrong when one attempts to be too accurate in holding the protective mask on the imaginary joining line. I find that by deliberately moving the cloud mask sufficiently back and forth, so as to allow a certain amount of the light from the foreground negative to actually spill over onto the territory reserved for the clouds, that it will be possible to avoid a strong white line. This white area is the customary tell-tale sign where the two negatives have been joined. The best way to avoid it is by doing what appears to be the wrong thing—allowing them to encroach slightly into each other's preserve. Please note that we say *slightly*. Naturally, if you over-do it you may obliterate and darken important details.

MARKING THE SKYLINE

After giving the proper exposure time, turn off the enlarging light but do not disturb anything as yet. Swing the red filter of the enlarger into the protective position and again turn on the enlarging light. With a soft pencil (preferably the Eastman Negative Pencil) make a few identifying marks on the sensitive paper outlining the skyline position of the previously-exposed foreground. It is extremely important that these identifying marks be placed *inside* the boundary lines of the previous exposure (See Fig. 57). These dots are only of a temporary nature to be used as a guide when dodging in the sky. They are absolutely necessary now but they will have to be rubbed off with your fingers during development immediately after the print has been placed in the developer. If you place the dots on an area of the print which has not been exposed to light as yet, they will prevent the light from reaching the emulsion, with the result that you will have an interesting set of nasty white spots to worry about. Another thing, there seems to be a conspiracy among manufacturers to equip every enlarger with a very dark and therefore most impractical red filter, through which nothing can be seen. Some filters are so dark that they are definitely useless when the lens is stopped down. As we all know, most enlarging papers are so insensitive to yellow or orange light that they can be exposed to a very bright "OA" safelight during development. Using that as our cue, it is evident that in some cases we can use an ordinary orange camera filter over the enlarging lens and no fogging *will result within a reasonable time,* especially with slow enlarging papers. The filter factor for film material has no con-

112

nection with the factor for a practically color-blind emulsion such as paper. Anyhow, I always use an ordinary orange filter and can see everything plainly and without any danger to the paper in the easel.

PUTTING IN THE CLOUDS

After making the identifying marks, turn off the light and remove the paper from the easel, placing it back in a paper envelope or similar safe location. (See Fig. 58.) Put the Outline Guide with the pencil tracing back in the easel. Remove the foreground negative and replace with the cloud negative. (See Fig. 59.) Adjust the cloud negative to the proper height and focus so that it will line up critically with the pencil tracing on the Outline Guide. This, of course, is very important in order to have perfect registration. When this is done, turn off the enlarging light and remove the Outline Guide from the easel, but do not disturb the position of the easel. Now take the partially exposed paper out of its protective envelope and replace it in the easel, making sure that the side marked "Top" is placed in proper position. Pick up the cut-out mask marked "Mask to cover foreground" and hold it over the area of the print which represents the bottom portion. Look for the marks which you previously made to identify the exact position of the foreground and these will be a safe guide when doing the dodging for the clouds. (See

Figure 58. The partially exposed paper, bearing the identifying dots which indicate boundary line of foreground, is removed to a safe place while the cloud negative is adjusted.

Figure 59. The foreground mask is used to protect exposed portion and is moved to allow overlapping of cloud area into foreground. Use pencil marks (Fig. 58) to guide position.

Fig. 58.) You are ready to begin, but if you are a bit uncertain just how to dodge, you can make a trial attempt with the orange filter in position. When doing the actual dodging, you must again bear in mind that a perfect "blending" will be much more easily achieved if you make sure that a certain amount of the lower portion of the sky negative is deliberately allowed to trespass into the foreground area. In other words, again allow the two to *slightly* overlap. After the proper exposure, develop the print for the standard time, place in the stop bath, fix—and check on the result.

If you have followed in detail what has just been described, it is quite possible that everything is perfect right from the start. (See Fig. 52.) However, if the blending is not exactly right, try to determine whether you should allow *more* or *less* overlapping. Also, it may be necessary to do some *extra* dodging for each negative, apart from the actual joining procedure, such as more printing-in time for the foreground, or the sky, or even printing-in for central sections. After all, if you want a fine print, you will have to resort to all of the manipulations called for in ordinary good printing technique, perhaps including flashing. In any case, whether corrections or additions appear to be necessary, mark them all carefully on the cut-out mask (See Fig 56), in order that your plan of action will be clearly before you. Combination printing does not require a great deal of resourcefulness, but it does call for being fairly wide awake and having a regular system of procedure.

Now, suppose that after several attempts you have finally succeeded in making a pretty good print but it is still not perfect and it is getting toward bed-time. In such a case, it is quite reasonable to use such a print and finish it up with spotting, perhaps even intensification or reduction, and then copy it with your camera. With such a master negative you can make all the perfect prints you want and flood the market without further trouble—that is, if you know how to make a good copy.

OTHER METHODS

Another version, of course, is to print both negatives onto a film, instead of paper. This film positive can also be put into perfect retouched condition and either copied by transmitted light, or placed in contact with another film and a contact negative made. With a little bit of imagination, dozens of methods will become apparent to you, but all based on the very simple method described here. If it seems

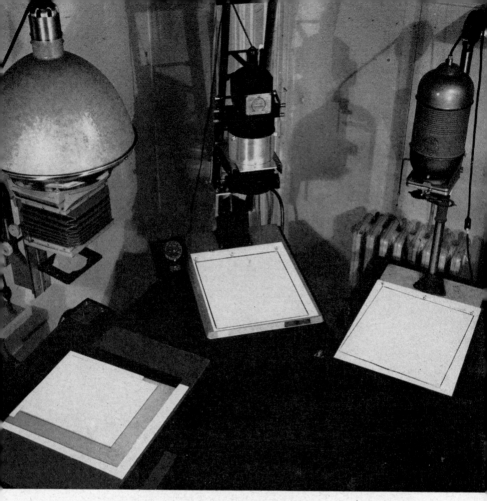

Figure 60. If you have more than one enlarger, the work can be simplified by placing a negative in each. The lines on the white mounts indicate the position of the easel (Figure 80) for each printing. Above, the sensitive paper in easel is in position for the first exposure under the enlarger to the left. This setup was used to print the picture "Beat! Beat! Drums" shown in Figure 89.

a bit complicated in the reading, be sure that it will not be so in the doing. If you had never ridden a bicycle before, imagine how impossible written instructions would appear to you when trying out the strange contraption in the back yard for the first time!

MULTIPLE ENLARGER MONTAGES

The picture "Beat! Beat! Drums!" which is shown on page 143 is actually the result of a montage of three negatives: a negative of the

Concord Minute Man, one of a Chesapeake Bay cloud and the last a negative of some of New York's Central Park overhead foliage. While this could be done in one enlarger in the way described previously, it is, of course, much simpler to do your montage work by using a separate enlarger for each negative. All you have to watch is that the contrast of the negatives is suitable to the paper and the enlarger.

By tracing an outline guide (Figure 53) and by using this to get the correct focus and outline for each negative, it then becomes a simple matter to put the paper in the easel and find the correct position for each printing-in by tacking down white mounts on each enlarger board, and tracing upon each mount an outline of the easel when it has been placed in the proper position under each negative. It is best to use white mounts, of course, with a strong black crayon so that you will have no difficulty in finding the correct placement in semi-darkness.

Figure 61. To print a portion of a negative many times, to complete a design or add foliage, etc., mark the successive easel positions on an old mount with heavy, black crayon pencil, so marks can be seen in the dim light of the darkroom.

Figure 60 shows the correct line-up of three enlargers for the actual making of the picture, "Beat! Beat! Drums!" with the easel in position on the white mount on the enlarger to the left for the first projection.

A USEFUL TRICK FOR SUCCESSIVE COMBINATION WORK

Sometimes we find it necessary to make two or three exposures from parts of the same negative in order to add or to change the outlines of the negative. For example, we may have on one corner of the print a few branches which look perfectly all right but which are not balanced by branches on the other side. Or we may simply wish to add to the size or extent of the foliage. A good trick in such a case is to first print the negative and then move the frame into a lower position, and repeat the printing of the top foliage, of course, in the meantime protecting the lower portion of the picture by proper dodging.

Move the easel as shown in Figure 61, utilize the white cardboard mount idea, outlining on the mount with heavy crayon the successive positions which the easel must occupy in order that the combination will finally be properly joined. It is amazing the amount of combination work which can be done through this same procedure. For example, if you study the picture, "Beat! Beat! Drums!" the foliage on the top of the print, which extends across the sky, actually was made from two or three small branches, but by successive printing part of the negative was made to appear as if the whole top area had been framed with branches at the time of taking the picture. (See Figure 89, page 143.)

CHAPTER XIV

PHOTOMONTAGE

THE word "Photomontage" is a comparatively new and fancy term applied to one of the oldest techniques in photography. Close to a hundred years ago, when our profession was just a toddling infant, O. G. Rejlander created a combination print from 30 negatives which demanded such technical skill and patience that only a handful of workers could equal it even today. I am, of course, referring to his "Two Ways of Life" which created a sensation when first exhibited in 1857.

Many modern practitioners limit the meaning of "Photomontage" to two processes; first, where several exposures are made on one negative (either deliberately planned or an accidental double exposure) and, second, printing divers negatives on to one single print. (Strictly speaking, combination printing of cloud and foreground negatives is Photomontage). However, in a broad sense, the term should include any and all possible methods of forms where we resort to combining two or more negatives or prints to make one final picture. This includes, therefore, what the French call "collage" and which we humbly label "paste-up," and of all the scores of available techniques, I definitely would suggest that you try this comparatively simple procedure before indulging in methods which call for the making of diapositives, or other tests of your photographic knowledge.

This chapter, therefore, will be confined to the making of a montage (the shortened word sounds better) by cutting out several prints, pasting them together, and copying them with a camera. While there are certain effects we cannot obtain by this method, it does offer to the average worker the greatest opportunity for creative work with a minimum of equipment. Personally, I will never forget the satisfaction I derived from doing a paste-up job when I was called upon to finish a picture of a gentleman who had passed away many years ago. A crude snapshot had been found showing the man comfortably seated with rolled up shirt-sleeves, and two affectionate children throwing their arms around his neck and shoulders. These same children, now grown up, desired to have a regular studio portrait of their father, all dressed up in suit and tie without complicated background. To their amazement, I had the final picture ready for them in a few days' time, and I vividly remember their sincere joy at the finished work and the awe with which they admired the "artist" who had drawn such a perfect new outfit on Dad. Little did they realize that all I had done was to get a friend of mine to pose in the studio in the same position as the original snapshot and then pasted a cutout of the old gentleman's head on the sturdy shoulders of my friend.

The finished montage, therefore, can be made to appear as an "unfaked" print; or it can be so fanciful and unreal that there is no attempt to fool anyone. It can be humorous, satirical, political, impressionistic or anachronistic. It can be used for pictorial or advertising purposes and, in capable hands, it can be as realistic as Jim Tully or as vague as Gertrude Stein, if I may be permitted to use such a juicy comparison.

Whatever you decide upon, remember that the more prints you are going to combine, the more work you will have to do. It would be best in the beginning to limit the work to two or three prints. Each picture, of course, will have its own peculiar problems, but if you follow me through with the making of the print under consideration, you will be able to adapt the system to your own satisfaction.

In addition to an Idea, here are the things which you are going to need:

Plenty of single weight glossy paper
Rubber cement (or a good substitute)
Small pair of scissors (for preliminary cutting)
A knife with a very sharp, fine point (such as a Bard-Parker
    #11 scalpel, with extra blades in case of breakage)
A stiff razor blade (single blade of the "Gem" type)
Block of fine sandpaper

Figure 62. Before beginning to make a photomontage, sketch the idea on paper to form a basis for selecting the parts for the finished montage.

Eastman negative pencil (to make outlines on glossy surfaces without endangering the print)

Large piece of glass (upon which to cut and paste the pictures)

A palette knife (or any flexible steel blade with no cutting edge, with which to remove prints that stick to glass or paper)

LOTS OF PATIENCE!

"ROSEMARY" is the outcome of combining nine prints (made up from four different negatives) and, naturally, entailed plenty of work. The idea of making a picture of the Civil War period came to me when I met a charming Southern lady. Several pictures were made and in one of them I secured the desired composition of the figure, but the facial expression was rather a bit cold for a lady from the Sunny

120

Figure 63. The composition in this picture is good, and in line with the sketch, but the expression is poor.

Figure 64. From another shot the head and shoulders were selected, reduced to proper size and cut out.

South (Fig. 63). On another negative, taken at almost the same angle, I found just the right expression (Fig. 64) and, of course, you will sense immediately what I was going to do: combine the pleasant smile with the graceful pose.

The main picture being decided upon, I made a rough pencil sketch (Fig. 62) to see what else was needed. I felt right from the start that I wanted to give the illusion the picture had been taken outdoors, preferably on a Southern estate. After a few modifications, I finally arrived at a design that called for a landscape scene with a distant light background and a railing which would be a link between a seated figure and the landscape. It was easy to locate a suitable landscape (Fig. 65) in the files, but for the life of me, I couldn't find a suitable middle-ground until I recalled the Fifth Avenue Public Library had an appropriate setting. So I dashed over with a small camera and in ten minutes I had my classical balustrade which might have been part of a grandiose estate (Fig. 66).

I was now ready to start the photographic printing. Realizing that it is always best to work with the largest size prints, I started

Figure 65 (above). From the files this print was selected to form part of the background. Two prints of this were made, one of them reversed and in addition, several separate prints were made of the foliage to block out sections of a tree, which otherwise would have appeared to grow out of the girl's head.

Figure 66 (below). The balustrade of the Fifth Avenue Public Library was photographed to provide a suitable middle ground and suggest a railing such as might be found on an old plantation. Two prints of this scene were needed.

Figure 67. A small print of some of the foliage is placed behind the head to block out the tree trunk, apparently growing from the girl's head. This is the first "rough" paste-up.

by making an 11 x 14 print of the figure of the girl, the center of
interest which would dominate the picture and which would be a
guide for the proportionate size of all other objects. (As a matter
of fact, it is advisable to make all prints even as large as 16 x 20
inches, so that the final picture can be reduced to a smaller size, the
reduction in size helping to hide any crude joining or other defects).
However, basing on the 11 x 14 print of the girl, I tried to estimate
the comparative harmonious sizes of landscape and railing. The "smil-
ing" head, of course, was easy to make up as it had only to be the same
size as the "serious" face. All these preliminary prints should be made
on any old paper—there is no sense using your best stock as these first
prints will never be entirely the right size or contrast. Thus, after enlarging a few prints representing the four negatives as planned in the
original sketch, I endeavored to assemble them by first cutting out
the figure of the girl and trying to arrange the suitable background
around it. From these first rough prints it was immediately noted that
the figure would have to be made larger; also that I was going to
need two prints from the "railing" negative so that it would extend

123

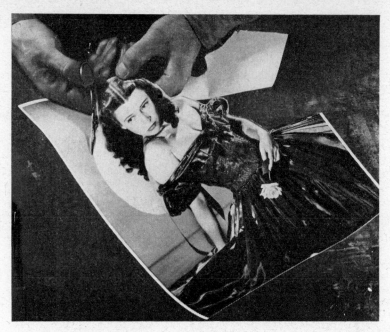

Figure 68 (above). After the exact sizes of the prints have been determined from the rough paste-up (Figure 67) the good prints are made and cut with small scissors. Leave a margin of about $\frac{1}{8}$ inch around all edges. This will be removed in the final trimming. Figure 69 (below). The cut-out figure is placed in position on the background and the outline traced with a negative marking pencil, which can be rubbed off without damage to the print. Do not press on pencil too hard. This alignment and tracing with pencil should be done to all prints so that only the final fitting remains to be done, before the pasting.

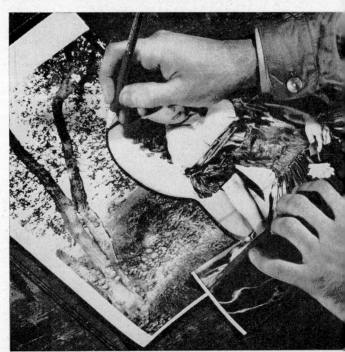

Figure 70. Rubber cement is applied to a sheet of glass and also to the prints, which are then pressed tightly together.

clear across the picture. In addition, I required five prints from the landscape negative; that is, two prints of the whole scene, one of them reversed, and three smaller prints of bits of branches which would be used to block out tree trunks growing out of milady's head (Fig. 67). In other words, nine prints were needed to complete the job. These final prints were printed on good single-weight glossy paper and care was taken that all prints would have the same tone, depth, and scale of contrast. This is very important—the prints should match in every detail so that they will appear to be printed from one negative when copied. Also, the proportionate size of each object was now carefully attended to, this being determined by the corrections which had been made from the first rough prints. And, as an extra safeguard, a duplicate was made of each print (eighteen in all), as it is quite easy to make a slip when cutting which would have stopped the whole job until I secured another print.

MAKING THE CUTS

After these new prints had been carefully dried (ferrotyping preferred), the first thing done was to cut out the figure of the girl (Fig. 68), leaving about ⅛ inch extra around the outline. This was

125

Figure 71. After pictures are mounted on the glass with rubber cement they are cut at one pressure using a fine scalpel. Cut steadily, don't hesitate.

Figure 72. In actual practice this final cutting is done only when the whole montage is pasted down. The unwanted part is then discarded.

laid on the background in accordance with the planned composition and an outline was traced with the negative pencil (Fig. 69). Any mark left by a negative pencil can easily be rubbed off with a clean cloth—but don't press too hard or the pencil may leave a depression. Following the pencil outline, the background was then roughly trimmed with the scissors, also leaving an extra ⅛ inch all around. This tracing with the pencil and rough trimming with scissors was done to the nine prints so that all prints were ready to be put together, only the edges needing careful adjustment.

GETTING THE JOINTS SMOOTH

The trick in all this paste-up work is to get the joints of the prints smooth and flat so that they will not be noticeable. The best way in which to do this is to securely fasten all the prints on a piece of glass with rubber cement, allowing a slight overlap (that is where the ⅛ inch extra trimming comes in). Then, with a very finely pointed knife (Bard-Parker #11), cut right through the prints to the surface of the glass with one push. (You must use glass in order to get a clean cut.) If the prints do not move during this cutting

126

Figure 73. After the unwanted part is discarded the
good piece is put in place, the fit should be perfect

process, after peeling away the unwanted trim of the top print, and
also discarding the unwanted part on the glass, you are going to find
that the remaining sections fit as tightly as a jig-saw puzzle. There is
nothing to equal this manner of fitting several prints into a perfect
whole.

Figure 74. Any imperfections in the fitting of the parts
can be corrected with the use of the spotting brush.

Figure 75 (above). After the montage is completed and spotted it may be copied in the usual fashion. Figure 76 (below). For those who find the newer method complicated, the older method may be used. This consists of cutting the parts separately, using a fine scissors or a razor held at an angle and backed by a glass plate. Before pasting up, the parts are sanded to a feather edge and these edges darkened with the spotting brush. The initial cutting must be extremely accurate to insure good fitting.

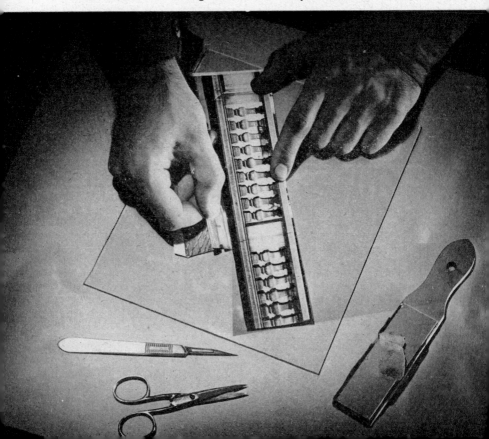

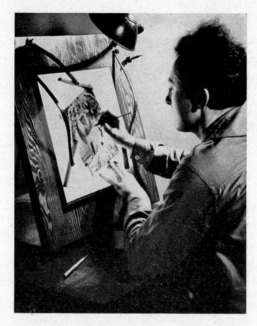

Figure 77. Any imperfections visible on the copy negative may be corrected by retouching with pencil, knife or dye before printing.

Therefore, I brought out a piece of 16 x 20 plate glass upon which I put a very thin coat of rubber cement, letting it dry for a few minutes. Then, starting with the landscape I also put the rubber cement on the back of the print (Fig. 70), the print and glass then being pressed together. When all background sections were fastened down, rubber cement was also brushed over any of the surface sections of the glossy prints where they would have to be in contact with the final superimposed prints, the balustrade and the figure of the girl. I have found it necessary to put both a coat on the glass and on the surface of the glossy paper, in addition to the back of the prints, in order to insure firm adherence during the critical cutting with the scalpel. However, it is comparatively easy to strip them apart later on, this having no relation with the permanency obtained when prints are fastened to *cardboard mounts* or *matte* surfaces. The palette knife is used to pry them loose if they should stick too much. If you have any trouble placing the prints together in their correct positions, you can help to overcome any difficulty along this direction in two ways:

129

ROSEMARY   Figure 78

place a strong light underneath the glass so that you can see through the prints while adjusting the top sections, or, place a piece of transparent cellophane over the pasted-down background; then place the cut-out over the cellophane and stick down on one corner, then slide out the cellophane and press down the rest of the cut-out into its proper place. Either of these methods or the two combined will assure perfect register.

All prints being rigidly secured, we are ready to do critical cutting with the fine scalpel. Be sure to cut at a steep (perpendicular) angle (Fig. 71)—not at a bevel or you will lose the benefits of this system. Then peel away the top ⅛-inch trim, pick up the part to be inserted and pull up the unwanted section from the glass (Fig. 72). Now return the insertion in the barren spot and the fit will be perfect (Fig. 73). You can leave the composite on the glass, finish up any rough areas with spotting (Fig. 74) and copy the montage in the regular manner (Fig. 75). (Copying can be done with a camera or with the enlarger itself). Or, if you do not want the montage to remain on the glass, and you have a dry mounting outfit, you can remove all the prints with the palette knife, clean off the rubber cement with a cloth, and place the pictures face down in perfect alignment. Then adjust the dry mounting tissue over the whole assembly and apply the necessary heat. This will enable you to pick up the whole picture and it is then ready for mounting and copying. After copying (which is simple if you have used glossy paper), you can either make the final print by projection or by contact printing, depending on the wanted size of the final print, always remembering that it is wise not to make the final picture any larger than the original "copy."

If some of the above manipulations sound a bit involved, you can always resort to the older method of cutting out all the paste-up parts separately, but this time at a bevel to the exact size with a sharp razor blade, scissors or scalpel, then thinning down the edges on the back of the cut-outs with sandpaper (Fig. 76). The edges are also darkened down with the spotting brush and cemented on to the background print and copied. While it is impossible to make the joints as perfectly fitting as in the first method, any errors can be rectified by retouching the copy negative and the final print (Fig. 77).

CHAPTER XV

HOTOGRAPHIC BORDER PRINTING

T HERE are many instances where a line or border around a picture would make for greater harmony and add a pleasing finishing touch. These borders can be simple or complicated in design. Where only a black line is wanted, many workers draw this in with pen and ink and while this manual procedure is quite often satisfactory, a better job can be secured through recourse to the photographic process. This is especially true if more than a black line is required, for then it is imperative that we do it by the printing and developing method.

MAKING THE EASEL

Before we start working on the border, it would be best to make a special easel. While in a pinch you can use any printing frame around your darkroom, this new easel is so easy to make and so useful for scores of other jobs that no darkroom should be without it. It can be made from seasoned wood, masonite or simply a very stout exhibition mount, depending on what material you have available. The one I use is made from a strong cardboard mount, slightly thicker than $\frac{1}{8}$ inch. The size should be a few inches bigger all around than the largest paper you intend to use; for example, an easel for use with 11 x 14 paper, would be approximately 13 x 16. Next, I cut out two strips of another piece of heavy mount, each strip being approximately $\frac{3}{4}''$ wide by 12" long. These strips are glued down along two sides of the cardboard mount, and the easel is completed. (Figure 80.) When the easel is being used in ordinary work, a piece of glass almost as large as the cardboard can hold the enlarging paper

132

down flat, both the paper and the glass being pushed securely against the two strips which act as a "stop." It is the simplest easel to use when it comes to evenly lining up the printing paper, and it is definitely unsurpassed where we wish to utilize the full size of the paper without white margins. However, today we are not going to use our home-made easel for straight enlarging work but as part of our equipment needed for making lines and borders on prints.

In addition to the easel, we will require the following:

Two pieces of glass, preferably same size as the picture.
A set of Kodak Mask Charts, same size as the picture, or any opaque paper. (If no Kodak masks are available, expose some printing paper to a strong light and develop until the paper is completely black.)
Rubber cement (or anything which will make the masks adhere to the glass).
A sharp knife (to cut clean edges in the masks).
A good straight ruler, preferably with a metal edge.
Some black lantern slide tape (not absolutely necessary but extremely handy to correct mistakes in cutting).

PRINTING A BLACK LINE WITH A WHITE BORDER

Our first problem is the making of a mask and countermask for the purpose of printing a black line with a white border around an enlargement, and our first job is to paste down masking papers on the two glass surfaces. Taking the first glass, put a thin layer of rubber cement on one side of the glass and let it dry. Also, put a coat of cement on the BLACK side of the masking paper and let that dry. After a few minutes drying, stick the mask and the glass together. A simple way of doing this without getting into trouble, is to first place a piece of wrapping paper or an old print on the cemented glass and then carefully tip the edge of the mask on to the corner of the glass. The wrapping paper will prevent the cemented surfaces of mask and glass from sticking together until you are satisfied that they are properly lined up. Then, after checking for perfect register, press down the corners firmly and slowly withdraw the wrapping paper from between mask and glass, pressing the two together from the center outward. The wrapping paper not being cemented, will not stick but is a guarantee against a slip of the hand. (This is also the best method for sticking exhibition prints on to cardboard mounts. See Fig. 81.) Go

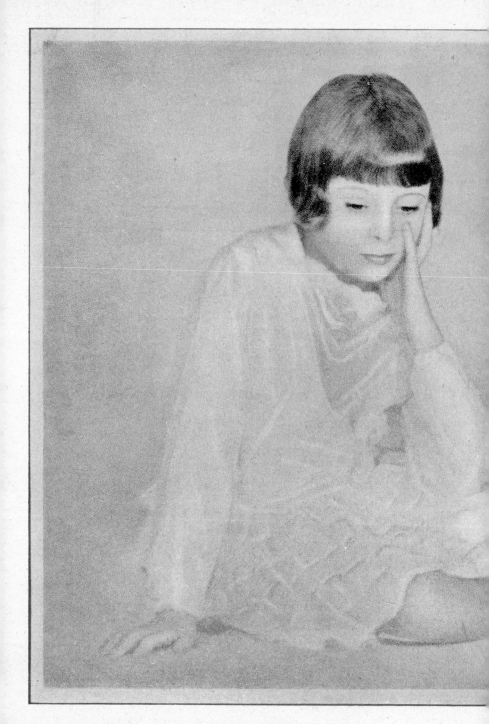

ORIENTALE
Figure 79

Figure 80 (above). The homemade easel should be constructed first. It consists of a cardboard mount on which has been glued two card strips to act as a "stop." The clear glass shown is for use in ordinary enlarging to hold the paper flat. The black arrow indicates the direction that glass and paper must be pushed to be in correct alignment. This type of easel permits the use of the full size of the paper, without the usual white margins and is easily made.

Figure 81 (below). Sticking the mask to the glass. A coat of cement is applied to glass and mask then allowed to dry. A piece of plain paper is put between mask and glass until alignment is right, when the paper is slowly peeled away with one hand, the other pressing the mask to the glass. Place black side of mask down. This method is also good for mounting exhibition prints.

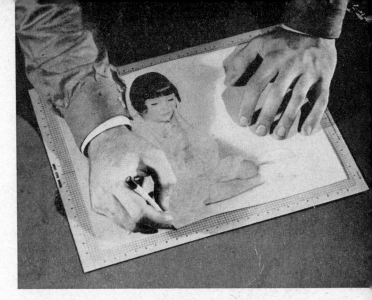

Figure 82. The size of the "A" mask is determined by placing a proof print on the Kodak mask and tracing the outline. This is then cut out with a sharp knife and a ruler, or straight edge. The cuts must be true.

through this procedure with the two glasses and two masks and mark them "A" and "B," respectively. We are now ready to cut the masks.

CUTTING THE "A" MASK

The first mask to cut ("A") is the one which will determine the size of the picture itself. I usually figure this out by having a rough proof of the picture available which I lay over the mask and then trace the exact size (Fig. 82). Having such a proof available allows exact determination of shape and size of the cut-out mask. As we are going to print a border on the print itself, it stands to reason that using an 11 x 14 size paper we will not be able to make the image much bigger than, let us say, 10 x 12. Using the sharp knife and steel ruler, I carefully cut along the 10 x 12 outline traced on the mask, which is very easy to do inasmuch as the paper is securely fastened to the glass. Be sure to cut at a perpendicular angle and with a clean sweep—don't fumble or hesitate once you start to cut. (If there should be any tendency for the ruler to move during the cutting process, I secure it to the drawing table with two small clamps, one at each end, the same as I do when making cut-out mounts for exhibition purposes.) After cutting the four sides all around, pull the 10 x 12 inside cut portion away from the glass which will leave only the outside masking rim

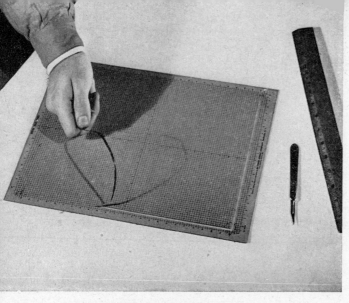

Figure 83. Finishing the "B" countermask. The mask has been perforated with the knife along two parallel lines. The cut portions are peeled from the glass leaving a clear space through which the light passes to print the dark line. The line is about 1/32 inch wide.

on the glass. (The rubber cement still adhering to the glass inside this rim should be cleared away by rubbing either by hand or preferably with a piece of clean cloth.) This mask gives the white border.

We are now ready to cut the "B" mask, the one which is used to print in the black line. We have to watch our step a bit here and measure everything carefully. This mask is going to be used AFTER the picture has been printed and will be placed over the print to protect the image when printing the black border. Inasmuch as we want a WHITE border between the picture and the black line, we must be sure that the "B" mask is slightly bigger all around than the 10 x 12 opening of the "A" mask. How much bigger depends on the width of the white border desired, and this can be anywhere from 1/16 to ½ inch. Generally speaking, the bigger the picture, the bigger the white border. For an 11 x 14 print, I would suggest a white border of 3/16 inch, although the border could be slightly larger on the bottom of the picture for composition purposes. Assuming that 3/16 is the width of the border we want, and that our "A" mask is cut to an opening of 10 x 12, the pencil outline we now trace on the "B" mask should be 10-3/8 and 12-3/8 inches. After this first line is traced, we now trace a second parallel line around it on the *outside*. This second line determines the *width* of the black line and should

138

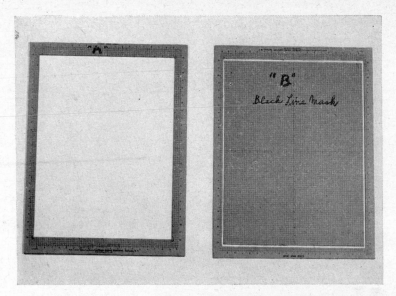

Figure 84. The "A" mask is used first and placed over
the sensitized paper on the easel and the exposure for the
negative given. It is then replaced with the "B" mask
and a separate short exposure (with negative removed) is
given for the line. The exposure may be made by flashing.

rarely if ever exceed 1/16 inch in width. Personally, I prefer the black
line to be slightly narrower—closer to 1/32 inch. After both lines
have been correctly marked, repeat the cutting procedure as for mask
"A." After cutting along both parallel lines, remove the thin ribbon
of paper which the cutting has produced, (Fig. 83), clean off the rubber cement from the exposed portions of the glass, and mask "B" is
also ready for use and we are ready to start printing (Fig. 84).

First, place a piece of paper on your home-made easel upon which
to focus, and on top of that place the "A" mask. Focus the image of
your negative so that it will be properly placed within the outline of
the "A" mask. After these preliminaries, remove the focusing paper
from under the glass and replace with the sensitized enlarging paper.
Be sure that your easel does not move at this stage of the game—
and, most important of all, make certain that both sensitized paper
and "A" mask have been firmly pushed against the two strips which
have been glued down to the easel to act as a "stop" (Fig. 85). If
you fail to line up paper and mask accurately, you will not obtain an
even white border or black line later on. The dark arrow on the easel
(Fig. 80) shows in what direction paper and mask must always be
pushed in order to secure accuracy.

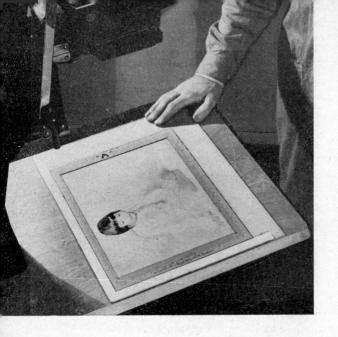

Figure 85. Making the original exposure. The picture is composed within the area of the "A" mask and the exposure made. The "A" mask provides a white border around the print. Both mask and paper must be firmly pushed against the stop to insure accurate registration in later printings, when the black line is added with a "B" mask.

PLACING THE COUNTERMASK

After making the correct exposure for the picture, remove the "A" mask and without disturbing the print on the easel, place over it the "B" mask. Again, check carefully that both enlarging paper and "B" mask have been solidly anchored against the cardboard strips (Fig. 86). You will now note that the "B" mask is actually a countermask which will protect the still undeveloped image on the paper but will allow light to go through the thin cut-out to form a black line. The light source for printing this black line can be the enlarger itself, but be sure to first remove the negative from the carrier. Inasmuch as this is really a form of flashing, I would prefer that you use the flashing set-up as suggested in Chapter X; that is, using a weak bulb for a light source. You can even attach the small bulb to the enlarger itself (Fig. 87), making sure that it is high enough to create an even exposure on the print. Or, in an emergency, you can quickly pull on and off the ceiling light—for a second or two exposure. In other words, anything that will give a good exposure will do, and the easel can be moved to any spot where the light is available as long as the sensitized paper and "B" mask do *not* move from their anchorage in the corner.

So that the black line will not overpower the image of the print.

140

Figure 86. Printing in the black border. As with the "A" mask, the "B" mask and the paper must be kept pushed against the stop on the easel to insure proper placement. The dark line should preferably be only as dark as the middle tones of the image. This line is printed-in by use of a flashing light, or enlarger light.

I would advise that you rarely make the line any stronger than the middle-tones of the picture itself. Only with a strong "low-key" picture with heavy black masses should you resort to a really solid line. Therefore, as a general rule, the exposure for the black line will only be a fraction of what is required for the picture itself (see Fig. 79 "Orientale").

The type and style of line borders you make depend on your taste and time. It stands to reason that any line border can be drawn such as an oval within a square, but this takes further planning and greater care (See Fig. 88).

The sharpness of the black line, whether oval or square, depends upon whether the paper mask has been placed flush against the enlarging paper or whether the mask is on top with the glass sandwiched in between. Naturally, the farther the mask is away from the sensitized paper, the softer the edges will be. I find that in using masks for very thin black lines, such as just described, it is often satisfactory to have the mask on top of the glass, whereas in masking black OUT-LINES, such as Fig. 89, it is usually best to have the mask in direct contact with the enlarging paper and the glass on top. Anyway, you

141

Figure 87. Using a single mask to print in a black border without a white edge. The image is printed first and then protected by the mask while the border is being printed in. Borders of this type should be dark enough to obliterate details of the image that is underneath. See "Flashing," Fig. 26.

Figure 88 (below). The mask for a more complicated type of line printing. This shows an oval within a square, a rather effective combination for some kinds of portraits.

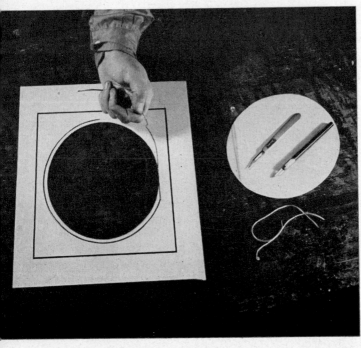

Figure 89

143

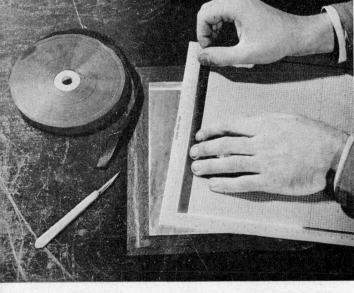

Figure 90. Lantern slide tape is an excellent mistake corrector if the knife has slipped. Here it is used to thin a border. Best done on glass with light underneath.

can easily determine which way you prefer it by merely reversing the mask and trying it both ways.

PRINTING A "FRAME" OR SILHOUETTE

The next method under consideration is really one of "framing" and not one of adding lines. In its elemental form, it consists of adding a solid black frame around the print without any white border. A direct way of doing that is to first expose for the print under the enlarger, then place an opaque cardboard over the sensitized paper, but leaving about 1/16 inch of the edges unprotected, and then turn on a "flashing" light. (Chapter X, Fig. 26). A superior way, however, is again to use a piece of glass to which is cemented an opaque mask. The glass and mask should be the same size as the final print, and, for this type of framing, only one mask is required. Through the use of a rough proof, decide what size and shape the black outline should be and trace this on the mask. You can make a simple black border, or you can make the opening the shape of a circle, an oval, a triangle, or whatever is required for the best composition of the picture. Solid black circles and ovals fit quite well around portraits and, with landscapes, quite often give a much needed third-dimensional effect. Also, very complicated designs can be made

144

creating the illusion that we are looking out of a window, doorway, covered bridge or whatever seems to fit the picture. Silhouette cut-out figures of trees or even people can often be introduced with realistic effect.

In making the black border around Fig. 89, it was felt only a simple outline was required except that two slight curves were introduced on the top of the frame. A pencil tracing was made on the opaque mask which was then cut with the knife in the usual manner. Then the *outer* rim of the mask was lifted from the glass, leaving the large inner countermask which was to protect the picture. To use this mask, print the image first as usual in the home-made easel, in this instance using the clear glass on top of the paper to hold it in place, (Fig. 80). After making the exposure, remove the clear glass and replace with the countermask. Here again, be sure that both paper and countermask are firmly pushed against the "stop" so that they are evenly lined up. Make the exposure by turning the room light on and off, and when the print is developed you will have the black outline around the picture. (See Fig. 87).

Of course, the above stunt can be accomplished by cutting out paper masks without being pasted on the glass, but usually it is very difficult to line up both paper and mask so that the border will always fall in the same place. If you are going to try this without the benefit of glass, then the best thing is to line up the mask on the enlarging paper with the help of the red filter on the enlarger. I don't recommend it this way, because while it sounds simpler, it is conducive to more waste of paper than you will relish.

We have been assuming that during all our figuring and cutting everything came out precisely as planned. However, don't be too amazed if you find that occasionally you may have cut a border too wide or too long, or perhaps the knife slipped a bit and almost ruined a mask. Here's where the lantern-slide tape comes in—correctly applied it will narrow a border to the right thinness or it will patch up any miscalculations of the knife. This corrective work is conveniently done over a retouching desk or, better still, over a glass opening built in a table with a light underneath. (See Fig. 90).

145

CHAPTER XVI

RETOUCHING WITH NEW COCCINE

NEW COCCINE is the greatest little darkroom assistant available to the photographic profession. At our command it will act as a dodger, reducer, intensifier or an opaque. In portraiture, it will make blondes out of brunettes, and high-key prints from low-key negatives. In commercial work, it will remove the shadows from interiors, brighten up dark pieces of machinery and lighten up or remove entirely distracting backgrounds. In pictorial work, it will eliminate the harsh contrasts between foreground and sky and it is indispensable in the handling of winter scenes where we have dark rocks and trees against brilliant snow. As I have often told the students, New Coccine puts that certain "latitude" in negative emulsions which the manufacturer so fondly hopes for.

It can be applied in such a manner that even a purist can look you straight in the eye, or it can be manipulated with the flourish of a painter for a decided pictorial effect. And, last but not least, it is equally useful for negatives of all sizes, from the small 35 mm. miniature up to the 8 x 10 or larger, being absolutely without grain or texture.

New Coccine is an inexpensive red dye which is readily dissolved in water and which is applied to the negative with brush or cotton. The application of different concentrations of the dye changes the density of any section of the negative so that all degrees of tones can be secured in the print.

I distinctly remember an unusual case where a professional photographer started to develop an important film in a tank which was

Figure 91. Five of the seven bottles shown contain different dilutions of New Coccine. The sixth contains ammonia and the last powdered New Coccine shown in its original container.

only partially filled with developer. After about five minutes he suddenly remembered that the film was only partially covered as the level in the tank was low. Of course, he immediately filled the tank to the correct level but the damage had been done. One-third of the negative was very thin due to under-development.

But by the clever use of New Coccine, he built up this thin portion to sufficient density so a print could be made which did not reveal a noticeable trace of the original error. Not every photographer will be faced with such a problem but it does illustrate the versatility of this simple red dye.

New Coccine should be in the kit of every photographer and I believe it would be if detailed instructions were more readily available. Unfortunately, most of the information given out is rather sketchy and after a few attempts the average worker puts his bottle away on a dusty shelf. It was about fifteen years ago that I bought my first bottle and during that period I believe I have worked out a system which is practical and which I hope you will give a *serious* try.

In addition to a bottle of New Coccine, (which contains 10 grams, or approximately 154 grains of red powder) you will need the following:

Six 2-ounce bottles (at the local drug store)
An eye dropper
A #3 Winsor Newton spotting brush (best for all-around work)
A dozen white blotters
Absorbent cotton
1 lb. 28% ammonia

Other items which it would be advisable to secure, although not absolutely necessary are:

A bottle of wood alcohol
A bottle of 10% Aerosol (or similar wetting agent)
A box of Q-tips (cotton swabs)
A #00 Winsor Newton brush (for small areas and delicate work)
An inexpensive magnifying glass—about 2x magnification—with a minimum diameter of 4"
A blue viewing filter or a piece of blue cellophane mounted in a cardboard
A Guillot (quill) pen for eliminating pin holes or making extra strong marks on the negative. This should be used carefully on the negative or it may scratch.

I am assuming that you have a retouching desk or viewing box; perhaps even a table with a glass-top desk and a light underneath. In an emergency any glass support with a light in back of it will do, but if you are a serious worker, you should buy or build a good desk.

PREPARING THE BOTTLES

Take the six 2-ounce bottles and mark them #1, #2, #3, #4, #5 and #6. This can be suitably done by sticking adhesive tape to the bottles and writing on the tape with a pencil or waterproof India ink. Put one ounce of water into each of the first *five* bottles. Distilled water is, of course, always best but usually not necessary. Now measure out ten grains (not grams) of the red powder and place the whole amount in bottle marked #5. (If you don't have a scale, use

148

a teaspoon filled slightly more than half.) The New Coccine will dissolve immediately and this powerful liquid is your stock solution.

Using the eye-dropper, take five drops out of bottle #5 and place them in bottle #1; then place ten drops from bottle #5 into bottle #2; twenty drops in bottle #3, and forty drops in bottle #4. In other words, you will have five different concentrations of dye, ranging in color from a light to a deep-red.

Now put into each of these five bottles 3 drops of the Aerosol (or other wetting solution). This wetting agent allows a more even penetration of the dye into the negative. This is especially necessary if the negative has been excessively hardened. Hardened negatives are always more difficult to retouch but they stand more abuse. If you have no wetting agent available, place instead a small drop of the 28% ammonia in each of the bottles, it will do the same work. This finishes the five bottles of New Coccine.

GETTING STARTED

In bottle #6, put one ounce of 28% ammonia to be used as a corrective eliminator in case you become exuberant and apply the New Coccine too strongly. Please treat the 28% ammonia with great respect—if you've never had a real whiff of a fresh bottle, don't try it now. As you use the #6 bottle, keep it to the side and not directly under the nostrils. However, ammonia being a gas, the contents of bottle #6 become gradually and finally useless; it is then necessary to get a fresh one-ounce supply from the larger bottle which should always be kept thoroughly stoppered. In case your dealer does not carry the 28% ammonia, you can try the regular household "clear" type, which, however, is not as effective, being about three times weaker. (See Fig. 91.) To get started, take the weakest color concentration, bottle #1, the #3 brush, blotter, Q-tip (or piece of cotton) and a graduate of clean water, and place these materials on the retouching desk (Fig. 92.) If you have a small negative, the magnifying glass will come in very handy although to many with good eyes it will not be absolutely necessary. For your first practice work, select a large negative or at least one that has a fairly large area to work on. If you are a landscape devotee, I would suggest that you pick a negative which has been under-exposed in the foreground or foliage areas, which means that when you print correctly for the sky the rest of the print is too dark. If portraiture is your main worry, try a nega-

149

tive where blonde hair needs to be brought out lighter, or there may be a large black shadow underneath a nose or chin which has to be modified.

Dip the brush into the clean water and get it thoroughly soaked, then draw it across the blotter several times to get it finely pointed and to discharge the excess water. It may be necessary to do this a few times in order to bring all recalcitrant hairs to a needle point. Also dip the "Q-tip" (or wad of cotton) into the water and squeeze it practically dry on the blotter. Hold this in your left hand to be used for wiping off or blending in excess moisture from the brush. When this has been done, you are ready to dip the brush into bottle #1. Remove the brush from the red dye and wipe it across the blotter in a turning motion. AT LEAST TEN TIMES. This will remove most of the excess red liquid and leave the brush slightly damp but nicely pointed (Fig. 93). This is extremely important, because a too-wet brush is one of the main reasons why so many fail to get satisfactory results from the New Coccine. A soaking wet brush slapped on to an unsuspecting negative will give you deserved trouble and a mild panic trying to prevent the liquid from running all over the place. The brush is ready to be applied to the negative when it is

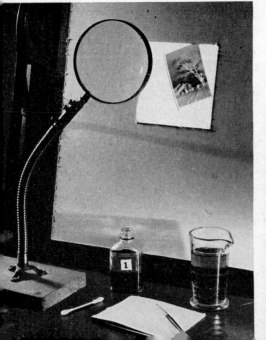

Figures 92 and 93. Begin with the weakest solution and have water, Q-tip, blotter, magnifying-glass and brush on the bench. The brush should be wiped on the blotter TEN TIMES before being applied to the negative. Keep fine point on brush.

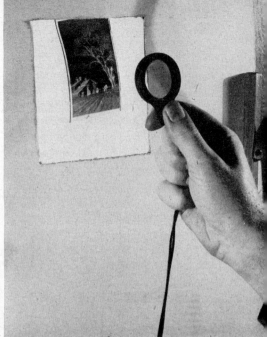

Figure 94. Hold brush vertically and move rapidly for 50 times. Wipe off excess moisture with a dampened Q-tip, or a piece of cotton held in left hand.

Figure 95. A blue viewing filter helps in judging the work. Make a final test by making a proof from negative. Blue cellophane also may be used.

just damp enough to keep a fine point—any additional moisture leads to difficulties.

The dye can be applied to both sides of the negative—but you should endeavor to always work on the *back* of the negative. The emulsion side is at best a delicate surface and easily damaged and only the experienced worker should attempt to work on this side. There are only about three instances where I would condone applying the dye to the emulsion side: First, in the case of 35 mm. negatives, where the back of the negative is so tough, or else no gelatin has ever been applied there so the New Coccine will not "take"; second, where after much work and repeated application, certain small spots of the negative become actually more transparent, the coating of the back seeming to wear off because of excessive wetting. It is then advisable to patch up this uneven density by carefully working on the emulsion side; and third, where a complete opaque background is desired and at times when negative material refuses to accept sufficient dye. However, the #5 bottle is so powerful that application of its contents on the back only is usually more than sufficient to completely hold back all light from the enlarger. Therefore, place the negative on the re-touching desk with the emulsion side toward the glass and the back (or shiny side) facing you. The almost dry brush should be applied in practically a vertical position. (See Fig. 94). This "head-on" angle of applying the brush insures better accuracy for if the brush is applied at too slanting an angle the dye is quite apt to overlap into unwanted places, with disastrous results. Don't press too hard on the brush—the point should not be flattened down. And now comes another important factor: Once the brush has been placed on the negative at the selected spot, it has to be KEPT MOVING FOR AT LEAST 50 TURNS. Don't lift brush off the negative; it must be in continuous contact. If you keep the brush moving you will eliminate practically all troubles of "lumping" or uneven spots. The movement of the brush can consist of small circles or ovals or up and down strokes, or a combination of all, but whatever you do, it is important that the movement be fairly rapid and that the strokes be comparatively small in any one direction so that the final result will be a perfect blend without overlapping into surrounding areas. In other words, the brush is moved and turned for a sufficient length of time so that all of the dye is completely and evenly absorbed into the gelatin without any further need for wiping off excess moisture or dye. If you should get careless, that is, get the brush too wet, you have in your left hand the slightly dampened Q-tip (or bit of cotton) to wipe off extra moisture. However, a careful worker will hardly ever have to resort to this wiping procedure, the Q-tip or cotton being more of a moral support or threat than an actual one.

USING THE #1 BOTTLE

After the first careful operation, you will note a very slight trace of red dye clinging to the negative. If your #1 bottle has been correctly mixed this mild application will have no noticeable effect on the printing result. Go through the whole procedure a second time, a third and even a fourth time. By now you should have a distinct red stain and it might be a good idea to place the negative in the enlarger for a proof. The chances are, however, that on the average negative it will take between five to ten perhaps twenty applications of the #1 bottle, before anything worth while results. The #1 bottle, therefore, has been deliberately made weak and you may lose patience but you should never get into trouble with it. It is a good safe dilution to start with so that when you reach for the stronger solutions later on you will know what to expect.

A trick that sometimes will be a time-saver in this work is the use of a blue contrast filter with which to check the actual retarding power of the red dye. To an inexperienced eye, the real strength of the red dye is at first difficult to estimate without making a proof. The blue filter helps to bring the red color down to a comparative monochrome in balance with the color of the negative. When we look through the contrast filter, the red becomes almost the same shade as the negative and we can judge easier how much density we have worked up (Fig. 95). If you don't have a blue viewing filter, a piece of blue cellophane will do just as well. Whenever you are in doubt, however, always resort to the making of an actual proof. After a few weeks of practice and more familiarity with the actinic value of the dye, you will be amazed at how close you can guess the right moment when the job is finished and ready for printing.

PROGRESSING

Naturally, after more experience you won't resort much to the #1 bottle—you will progress to using the #2 bottle which is twice the concentration and, therefore, twice as powerful but also more dangerous to use. Then, after a few days more, you will perhaps be confident enough to begin using the #3 and #4 bottles. The dye in these bottles is really quite strong and striking effects can be obtained in a short time. These two bottles are my favorites for usual work, but please don't try them right away. Stick to the #1 and #2 bottles for a while until you can do it in your sleep.

Here is how I use the different bottles:

#1—to practice with and to learn the system—only for small areas with brush.

#2—to get a little faster result but still very safe—for small areas with brush.

#3—for really serious work—speedily done with brush or cotton—quite dangerous to use, however.

#4—very dangerous to use but my favorite for quick work with brush, pen or cotton. Eliminates pin holes and backgrounds easily—good for vignettes and general strong intensification.

153

Figure 96. This is a straight print on normal paper. Compare this flat, muddy original with Figure 97, on the opposite page, which shows the changes that were made with the application of New Coccine to the negative. All areas are pepped-up, clouds are put in, figures made to stand out, the texture of walls changed and the foreground altered. There was no dodging during printing. The picture is the work of New Coccine.

#5—the stock solution—used for replenishing the other bottles —or for an immediate elimination of the whole background—a fine opaque that doesn't flake off. Never use this bottle for ordinary work.

#6—the ammonia for removing excess dye either in thin layers or completely—only safe for small local areas. NEVER TO BE USED ON EMULSION SIDE OF NEGATIVE.

New Coccine applied with a very fine brush or a fine quill pen such as a Guillot is unexcelled for eliminating pin holes or for putting in an extra bright highlight for zip and dash.

After you have applied the right amount of New Coccine, it is always a good idea to wipe off the negative with a cleaner. A good all around cleaner for both negatives, glass and condensers is made up of 9¾ oz. of wood alcohol to ¼ oz. 28% ammonia. Use a bit of cotton, China silk, washed rayon or old linen handkerchief to apply the cleaner. These materials are best and should not scratch. For use on negatives, dip the cleaner on to the cloth and let it evaporate a few sec-

154

Figure 97

onds; don't apply it too wet or it may remove some of the silver. Swab the negative to remove any bits of film base which might have become loose through constant wetting and which will leave disagreeable little white spots to be removed on the print. These will show up especially if you use a condenser enlarger—those who use a diffuser type of light do not have much to worry about.

If you have kept the brush or cotton on the dry side while applying the dye, and then at the finish, followed up by swabbing the negative with the alcohol-ammonia cleaner, the whole surface of the negative will be dry and ready for printing within two or three minutes' time. The alcohol helps to evaporate all remaining moisture. If you are in a great hurry, even this period can be shortened by drying the negative over an electric bulb.

ALTERING THE AVERAGE LANDSCAPE

You will note from Figures 96 and 97, what can be done to an average landscape negative. The scene was taken on an early spring day. The picture has good composition but needed tones and gradations—a general pepping up in all areas. Also, the sky was disappointing and without any clouds to speak of. In any good picture we must have some area which stands out and naturally in this case this would fall on the space between the houses and the tree, including the two boys. The quickest way to create a center of interest is to make it contain the strongest highlights, preferably contrasted against shadows. There is nothing like a "light" spot to catch and hold the eye. So the dye was put on rather strongly just above the sky line between houses and tree and around the boys. After that the rest of the sky was worked up with clouds, around the chimneys and through the foliage. The trunk of the tree was strengthened in a few well-chosen spots. If you think that you have no real knowledge as to what areas to pep up, you can always play safe by merely strengthening or locally "intensifying" highlights which are already present in the negative. By adding extra density, you will automatically get a greater gradation of tones without sacrificing artistic integrity. All you are doing is bringing out more forcefully what is already there.

The houses were flat and dull so the next thing was to separate the gradation between the black roofs and the brick walls. This was easily accomplished by putting on repeated layers of dye over the wall surfaces only. Then in order to liven them up more and give the walls

156

Figure 98. If you do not desire to work on the original negative, a piece of cleared film may be attached to the back of the negative. The negative emulsion should be kept outside. Stick the two together with lantern slide or scotch tape. If a mistake is made the cleared film can be washed or discarded. You must use film as ordinary celluloid without a gelatin coating will not take the New Coccine. When printing by contact, or enlarging, the negative emulsion should face the emulsion side of the paper, just as is done normally.

more "character" I deliberately put the New Coccine on in heavy uneven streaks so that sections would seem more weatherbeaten. In this case, an even "blending" was not wanted as I was not trying to

157

Figure 99. New Coccine may be applied to large areas with a tuft of cotton which has been pressed on a blotter 10 times before being applied to the film. It should be kept moving for 50 turns to insure an even application. Repeat until sufficient strength is obtained.

hide the fact that something had been done to the negative. The last thing was to energize the foreground by accentuating and changing the dull ruts. Through all this work, I took good care to keep the applications away from the edges of the negative. The result was that when a STRAIGHT print was made the picture dodged itself slightly darker all around and made its own framing.

For those who have fairly large negatives, 3¼ x 4¼ or larger, or in any event if you feel a bit timid, there is a way in which you can learn to apply the New Coccine without getting into trouble. Take some unexposed film, preferably cut film, and fix it out completely in hypo, wash and dry. Attach this clear film base with lantern slide or scotch tape to the negative you wish to alter. (See Fig. 98). From now on you do all the retouching work, not on the negative itself, but on the attached new base. This will give you more confidence. In case you make a serious error, discard the clear piece of film and attach a new one. Cleared film must be used as plain celluloid has no gelatin coating to hold the dye. Figure 99 shows this process in use, the negative and clear film base being attached together on four sides. When printing the negative in the enlarger, place the emulsion face down as usual, keeping the attached film base on top in the carrier. While working on a supplementary film base is not quite as accurate as working directly on the negative, it certainly is a safe and sound method and in many instances will do all that is required. Figure 99 also shows how very large areas are covered with a piece of cotton. Fold the cotton into a small pad and tip the mouth of the bottle on to the cotton. Press the saturated cotton on to the blotter ten times in order to eliminate excess moisture, and apply it to the negative in a rapid motion of about 50 turns. In other words, the same technique of the brush is applied to the use of the cotton. The left hand again is on guard with another bit of dampened cotton to take up any excess moisture you failed previously to eliminate on the blotter. Comparing Figures 100 and 101, you will note that smoke was put in, that the background was completely altered and that the highlights in the face have been built up and the whole face dramatized.

REMOVING EXCESS DYE

Now supposing that you did put on too much dye or in the wrong place, what to do? If the WHOLE job has to be removed the safest method is to place the film in a tray of water and leave it there for several hours. No matter how strong the dye, eventually water will remove it, even if it should take 12 hours. If you are in a hurry however, place the film in a solution of any one of the sulphites; potassium metabisulphite, sodium bisulphite or sodium sulphite. I usually measure out ½ oz. of the chemical to 8 ounces of water and this works satisfactorily. Whenever you place a negative in this solu-

159

Figure 100. This is a straight print from the negative that produced the picture shown on the next page (Figure 101). New Coccine was used to put in the cigarette smoke, strengthen the facial planes and intensify the skull structure, alter the background and dramatize the picture. A comparison will show the improvements which have been made through the use of this simple red dye, applied as described.

Figure 101

tion, be sure to give it at least five minutes washing afterward, as this will eliminate any possible after-stains.

LOCAL CORRECTIONS

However, for average LOCAL corrective work, you will find the 28% ammonia the best of all. The ammonia is applied with a brush in the same manner as the New Coccine. Wet the brush, dip into the ammonia, wipe it thoroughly on the blotter first, then apply to the negative. NEVER APPLY THE AMMONIA TO THE EMULSION SIDE OR YOU WILL RUIN THE NEGATIVE. With a Q-tip (or piece of cotton) wipe off any excess ammonia from the negative. Sometimes I deliberately apply the New Coccine a bit too strongly and then work in soft gradations by "reducing" the density with gentle applications of the ammonia.

INTENSIFYING NEGATIVES WITH NEW COCCINE

Sometimes when a negative lacks printing density all over and yet it might be dangerous to intensify it because of the possibility of grain, soak it first in plain water for about 5 minutes. In the meantime, pour the contents of bottle #3 in a tray and then place the negative in this solution. Keep it rocking and in a few minutes it will have absorbed a complete coating of red dye. How long you leave it in there will depend on how much printing strength you wish. When you believe it has sufficient depth, hang up to dry. Afterwards, you can soften down excessive highlights by reducing locally with the ammonia. If you have over-done the complete job, remove all of the dye either by washing or by immersion in the sulphite bath. Another version of this method, is to coat the negative front and back with rubber cement to protect certain areas which do not need strengthening. After drying, the rubber cement is easily rubbed off with the fingers.

USING ON POSITIVE TRANSPARENCIES

New Coccine can also be used on positive transparencies to eliminate white areas or to give a complete dark background prior to making a new negative. It can also be used on paper negatives, but here it has to be used more cautiously and greatly diluted. The effect on paper is more drastic than on film.

162

At first the use of a red material may seem to be a drawback when working on black-and-white negatives, but in many cases you will find this an advantage. For one thing, you always *know where you are* when putting it on and this is very helpful when working on small negatives. Many of the other dyes on the market for this kind of work, which appear to be of neutral shades, are much harder to work and do not always dry the same color but vary in tints from purple to black, which can be very disturbing. In addition, some of these dyes will dry down much darker after five minutes' time than when initially applied. If you do wish to use a neutral dye, one of the best is that put out by the Spotone people and sold under the name of "Silver Black." It can be used under the same principles as laid down for the New Coccine. A neutral dye such as "Silver Black" does have an advantage when used in conjunction with a great variety of papers. Some papers have a different color sensitivity and naturally a red dye might have erratic results with some of them. Therefore, when using New Coccine be sure to make all your proofs on the same brand and grade of paper as will be used for the final print.

THE ESSENTIAL POINTS FOR SUCCESS

Here are the essential points to remember which will insure success right from the start:

Don't use any stronger bottle than you have control over!

Always use a blotter first—never put the brush on the negative directly without first wiping it, no matter from what bottle you work. A really wet brush spells trouble right off.

The brush should be wiped about 10 times, and should be just wet enough to keep its point.

The brush should not be pressed hard—if you push so hard that the point is completely flattened out, you are doing it wrong. About the only time it is permissible to flatten out the point is when big general areas are being covered.

Once the brush is applied to a spot, keep it moving (revolving

163

in circles and ovals) at least 50 times. This is a guarantee against uneven spots.

Apply many thin layers for a perfect blend.

Try to do all the work on the back of the negative. Don't use the emulsion side unless absolutely necessary.

One thing New Coccine will not do is to take the place of the retouching pencil, except when used on very large size negatives. When it comes to the very finest detail work, the pencil is still supreme. This is because the pencil can be brought to a finer point and therefore can penetrate better into smaller spots. But in all cases where the point of the brush can be kept within the confines of a given area, I resort to the use of New Coccine. For one thing, no matter how big the magnification, there will never be any grain or texture visible. It is also superior to the old method of working up a negative or transparency via the ground-glass method. While ground-glass, pencil and chalk are extremely helpful, they have too many drawbacks as compared to New Coccine. Ground-glass and chalk lead to lots of spotting on the final prints. It is inaccurate and difficult to use on small negatives and almost useless in a condenser enlarger, and there is a limit to the amount of density which can be built up.

CHAPTER XVII

PICTURES TO MAKE YOU THINK

To the person who has an open mind and who is interested in life in all its phases, there will never be a time when there is not an opportunity to take a picture. I would regret very much becoming a "one-sided" photographer who is interested in only one type of subject matter or one type of presentation.

Many amateur photographers may only want to take "beautiful" things but I like the healthier viewpoint of the professional, who can find something interesting and even inspiring in practically any subject material.

Never let anyone decide for you the kind of pictures you should take—unless you work for that person! If at the present time you have no definite preferences, go and take the things which interest you the most. After awhile you will find your natural curiosity will widen your horizon and even the most commonplace objects will become fascinating. Study the photographic magazines, visit exhibitions of pictorial, news, portrait, and documentary photography and you will soon get a balanced perspective which will enable you to select the type of pictures you like to make. At the same time you will learn to tolerate and even secure inspiration from work which you yourself would not care to do at the *present* time. You can never tell what you are going to prefer five or ten years from now.

For the above reasons the pictures and comments on the following pages have been selected to show a wide variety of subject material which runs the gamut from "candid snapshots" to professional portraits.

This photograph was taken deliberately for advertising purposes. Mr. Belden is very well known as a Western rancher, and incidentally as an excellent photographer for the last 30 years. Pictures of him were needed in connection with an advertising campaign and I was asked to do the job. My first impression of this gentleman was one of straightforward friendliness, and it was my endeavor to try to catch that impression, at the same time maintaining the Western touch. To give the picture punch, only spotlights were used, with no retouching of any kind whatsoever. Because the lighted cigarette is against the dark background, the smoke was caught in a natural fashion and required no manipulation to bring it out. To get Mr. Belden to assume a natural at-ease pose, he was asked to lean against the wall. The picture was taken while he was engaged in conversation and actually answering a question. A slight amount of flashing was done during enlarging in order to equalize the darkness of the backgrounds. The final picture was printed on glossy paper and ferrotyped. A 5 x 7 camera with a 6.8 Dagor lens was used.

Everyone knows that New York City is an inexhaustible treasure chest of pictures, which might well be said of practically any large city. With its big buildings, large parks and millions of people of all types, the photographer is surrounded by a photographic paradise where he can swing from pictorial to documentary work in five minutes' time. I had noted this particular picture for two or three months in advance of the actual taking and incidentally it is located within about one good size block distance of the picture entitled, "Two Ladies"—which merely goes to show the variation possible by merely changing a viewpoint. However, at the time when I first noted the scene the sky was dull and cloudless, and the absence of sun made it very dull indeed. But I had been struck by the unusual contrast between the tiny weatherbeaten pine and the luxurious modern skyscraper hotel in the distance. Somehow, the two of them to me were a wonderful illustration of how completely paradoxical New York can be within a stone's throw. So I kept the picture in mind but wanted a good sky and sunlight. Then one day about the middle of July, in the afternoon, when the sun was just about right for the viewpoint, a thunder storm began gathering over the city. I have noted for many years that the finest, most unusual and striking cloud formations are available either just before or after a storm, so I immediately grabbed my camera and rushed in a taxicab up to the spot I had previously selected, and by placing the camera on the ground itself and close to the small tree, I gave it the illusion of being of much bigger size than it actually is. (As a matter of fact, some of my students who later tried to find this "big tree" practically were stepping over it all the time and didn't know it because they did not take the worm's eye view necessary to see it.) Within a few minutes the storm began to break and yet there was still sunshine coming through, but with threatening, fast-moving clouds in the background.

The clouds traveled so fast I really managed to make only one exposure before the whole scene changed; the sun disappeared and a different cloud formation set in which, plus the rain that began, made it impossible to make any further exposures. I was fortunate in having caught the strong white cloud on the tree side which offset very nicely the towering building to the right. The picture is a straight print with the exception that the foreground has been somewhat dodged in.

The picture of my friend John, taken with his favorite pipe, was an informal portrait which also turned out to be quite a successful exhibition picture. John is not a particularly large or rugged individual but he does like the outdoors, and by having him put on his suede jacket, loosening the collar and removing the tie, we got a rugged effect. Secondly, by placing the head very close to the top of the paper we give an impression of larger stature. The original print of this was made on a buff stock with a slow chloro-bromide emulsion and developed in a pyrocatechin developer.

THE RODEO

The ideal way to have taken this picture would have been with a 4 x 5 camera with a focal plane shutter and a 10" lens. At the distance from which I had to take this shot a large size image could thus have been obtained plus the advantage of using a fast shutter speed in order to stop the action. As it turned out, I was quite unprepared to see this particular demonstration of Western skill, and it was merely by chance that I happened to pass the show. In addition I also happened to be under orders by my old friend the Doctor to relax for a few weeks so I even found myself, unusual as that may be, without a camera. However, a friend of mine did have a 2¼ x 3¼ camera with a shutter speed that fortunately went up as high as 1/400 of a second.

After watching a couple of the runs of the horsemen and the steers, I could see that the animals more or less ran in the same pattern; when the steer was loosened, he somehow knew he was going to be chased, and he ran as quickly as he could toward the fence, where he sensed that the lassoer would have a difficult time catching him. I, therefore, placed myself in the position which I felt would be the best spot to shoot everything at top action. Unfortunately, it meant I had to be a long distance away which gave an image on the negative about the size, if not slightly smaller than a 35 mm. negative. That is why, during the whole hour of this show, I was so fervently wishing I had my 4 x 5 camera and the long focal lens with me.

However, under the conditions, I believe I caught a very good bit of action, and in order to give the picture an extra pictorial touch —made the final picture by the paper negative process.

171

This charming art student was taken on one of the beaches of Cape Cod while an actual school of painting was in progress. Here, again, the use of a filter would not have been of much consequence inasmuch as the sky was of the pale variety which does not lend itself to filtering, especially when shooting against the light. When shooting against the light, it is very difficult to get shadow detail except through the use of a flashlight attachment, which in this case, was not used simply because my miniature camera did not have this arrangement. However, when it was decided to make up the print, the rhythmic figure of the young artist was given more detail through the use of New Coccine, as was also the little model who sat so patiently on the small stool. New Coccine was also used to eliminate or subdue the small boats offshore in the background. To give the sky its "filter effect," flashing was resorted to. In this instance printing-in would have been anything but advisable due to the dense, grainy sky on the negative which might have led to showing graininess if it had been printed through onto the paper.

EXPRESSION

"Expression" is a real candid shot taken without any preliminary posing and on the spur of the moment. In addition, it was taken with a 3¼ x 4¼ camera, from which only a small portion of the negative was utilized. While it may not be a perfect picture, I have always felt it was one of the most difficult that I have taken. I had gone to a small outdoor amusement park and was carrying my camera with shutter cocked and correct lens ópening in case anything unusual happened along. It was a late summer's afternoon and I had set the shutter speed at 1/100, which is the minimum required to stop action in such an instance. The lens opening was approximately $f6.3$. From quite a distance I could see a group of people watching something and as I got a little nearer, I put my camera under the outstretched arm of a person in front and managed to take the picture. These five were, of course, the main interest, but to secure merely what I wanted the picture had to be cropped practically to 35 mm. proportions as the rest of the negative showed a confused group of people. I had to guess-focus for the distance and I was pleased to note that even in the 14 x 17 enlargement the picture still stood up fairly well. Of course, with the comparatively wide aperture on a 135 mm. lens, the background was somewhat spotty, but this was later toned down. What interested me about this picture was the fact that the five people included seem as though they were looking at something rather startling or at least which would give pain or fear. Even the boy at the left with his upraised left arm seems to be in the act of warding off something which has frightened him. When I took this picture, I was not fully aware of all details, but I was amused later to find the range of expressions on these five faces came merely from watching a man oiling a miniature locomotive.

176

While New York has many skyscrapers, the one which has always fascinated me the most is one of the oldest—the Woolworth Tower. With its Gothic appearance it reminds me of a gigantic church, a veritable cathedral of commerce. Of course, I had seen the building many times before but I never had been actually tempted to take a picture of it until one time I happened to pass underneath the old elevated railroad and I saw this particular framing. From then on, I made up my mind to really take a picture of my pet skyscraper. However, the first time I attempted to get the most desirable viewpoint I had to stand in the middle of a busy street and the traffic made it more than hazardous, so I decided to come back on a Sunday. About a week or two later I attempted it again on the Lord's Day when downtown New York is deserted. I had no trouble whatsoever finding the correct position, but I ran into another snarl. There were no clouds. It seemed rather foolish to photograph a skyscraper without clouds but at the same time I also realized that perhaps it would be many a day before I could come back. Naturally, in such a case I decided that I would print in a cloud from another negative. When you know ahead of time that you are going to print in a cloud negative, it is sometimes much easier to let the sky portion of the basic negative become over-exposed. Therefore, when I took the picture, I used no filter whatsoever, so that the sky on the original negative is quite dense and opaque, which means when it is printed straight, the sky behind the building is very whitish. This made it much easier later on to double print the correct cloud negative because no dodging, to protect the enlarging paper from becoming dulled by a transparent sky, had to be done when printing the building itself. This left the paper in a nice white condition to receive the second exposure from the cloud negative. Of course, the proper cloud negative had to be found which fitted around the skyscraper in a graceful pattern, and finally the right combination was found by using only a small portion of the entire cloud negative. "Skyscraper" was, therefore, made from two negatives and was basically done in the same manner as combination printing described in Chapter XIII. The camera used was vest pocket size, placed on a tripod.

TEXTURE

This picture was made in a class demonstration to show students the basic principles of bringing out texture in materials. The rendition of texture basically depends on two factors—one, the material itself and two, and most important, the direction of the light at the time of the exposure. If you want to bring out texture in faces, in snow, in cloth or in any substance, the simplest way to do so is to arrange your light so that it either gives you a cross or back lighting. If you take pictures under flat lighting conditions, expect to get flat pictures. If you take pictures against the light, you will have brilliant results. Of course, you must be careful that the light is properly balanced. Outdoors, this may be difficult, although the light may be controlled in various ways through the use of reflectors, with the help of a flashbulb, shortening the time of development of the negative, by using New Coccine or, perhaps, a combination of all these methods. Indoors, with artificial light, the experienced photographer finds no difficulty in balancing the light.

The picture "Texture" is a straight enlargement, the set-up having been taken with one light in a low position, to give cross lighting and a second light on top of the cloth, in order to balance the shadows in a proper manner. The strength or power of the lights is not important in itself; in this instance, two 500 watt bulbs in reflectors were used. The cloth, a piece of satin, was placed on the floor and so manipulated that an interesting composition was secured. Many fascinating designs can be created indoors with simple materials and provide an excellent artistic and technical exercise for anyone who has a desire to get into professional photography. No retouching or alteration was resorted to on the negative and the final print was enlarged on No. 2 glossy paper and ferrotyped.

DISMANTLED

This could be classified as an industrial shot with a pictorial slant. The picture was taken of a coal mine which had finally more or less out-lived its usefulness and had been abandoned for more productive pastures, if such an expression could be used in connection with coal mining. However, my coal friends tell me that it is always more pleasant to use the term "dismantled" in such an instance. While wandering through the old plant and clambering up and down the black hills which surround such places, I finally found a spot where I could get a foreground framework in order to frame the plant in the background. This picture, too, was printed on glossy paper and the edges darkened down, especially in the foreground, in order to give it more depth. The picture was taken with a 3¼ x 4¼ camera on a tripod, stopped down to $f32$, so that both foreground and distance would be sharp. Always remember that the bigger the enlargement is going to be the more you have to stop down and the more critical the focusing has to be. A person who makes small pictures, that is, up to 5 x 7 or 8 x 10, doesn't have to be one-tenth as careful as the man who makes 14 x 17 and 16 x 20 prints. From an economical sense and perhaps for other reasons there may be some justification for trying to make the big size prints unpopular, but there is one thing certain—that to make a good big-size print you have to start off with a good negative. Perhaps this is one reason why the big-size prints are usually made by the more experienced workers, the newcomers rarely having a negative that can stand decent enlarging beyond 11 x 14.

This is an honest-to-goodness candid shot taken at the last World's Fair in New York. Of course, the best candid shots are always posed, but when you are out hunting with your camera you cannot always bring with you the proper models to get just what you have in mind.

I feel sure that thousands of visitors to the Fair will recall the rather gigantic statue of the star-gazer, which was placed near the Trylon and Perisphere. Somehow that big boy standing there all by himself seemed to impress me with a bit of the egotism of the average man, and I wanted to make a picture in which Mr. Man would be in his proper place.

The day I took this shot I was fortunate in seeing two stalwart ladies coming down the road with a very positive stride. Instinctively I felt that somehow they were the type who should be able to control almost any situation without too much trouble. I waited until they had passed and then placed my camera on the ground and took the shot while they were comparatively close, so that their figures would loom large in comparison to the statue.

The picture was taken with a 2¼ square reflex camera at about f8, 1/200 of a second and is a straight enlargement.

THE BOSS

This particular picture is perhaps more in the line of an informal snapshot, but because of the interesting character and the unusual background it is of more interest than pictures of this type generally turn out to be.

This gentleman happened to be in charge of a construction gang and seemed so ruggedly healthy and tanned, that with the addition of an evidently perpetual cigar in his mouth, I could not resist the temptation to take a shot of him. By darkening down the edges, the interest was kept concentrated on the figure of the man and in that manner the picture was lifted out of the snapshot stage. The print was selenium toned to a warm brown.

184

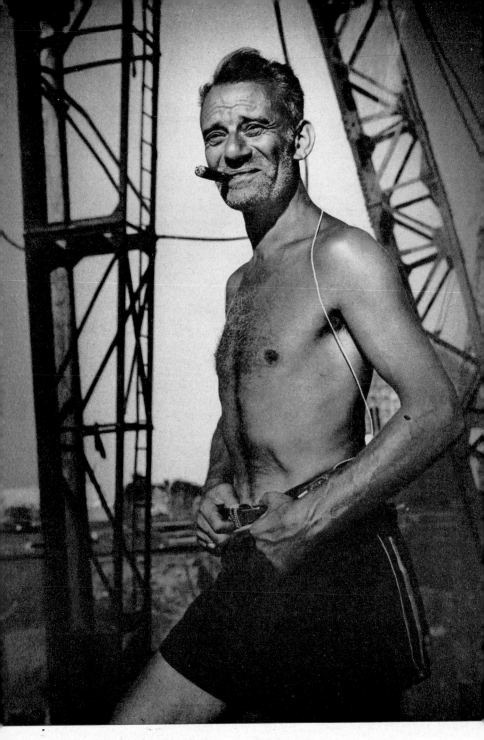

. One of my favorite hobbies outside of photography happens to be hiking and some of my most enjoyable pictures have been taken on such trips. As a matter of fact, in case you have been rather unfruitful in producing pictures on your vacation trips, may I suggest that in the future you try driving to an area, then leaving your car parked all day and doing the rest on foot.

This particular picture was the result of a very pleasant hiking trip with an old friend of mine. We had climbed up to the top of Mt. Washington on a rather sultry day and reached there about noon, when my friend suggested he would like to have his picture taken standing looking down toward the hut of the Appalachian Mountain Club. This picture was taken more or less as a record shot for him because with lack of good light and a dull sky, it would not lend itself to very much except as a record print. But more than that, the film pack with which it had been taken was light struck, and other troubles happened to the negative which made it anything but good technically.

Both with an idea to please him and also to show in a class demonstration the possibilities of the paper negative process, I decided to use this rather poor negative and make it into an exhibition picture. The first thing I did was to determine the mood of the picture. Somehow I felt that my friend, standing at the end of a cliff looking down, might be a wandering boy coming home to Mother or something of the sort. While the Appalachian Mountain Clubhouse will possibly hold 40 to 60 overnight guests, from the distance where we stood it might have been a small hut. Thus, having determined the mood, the rest was comparatively simple. I decided that if he were going to be coming home, it would be more dramatic if he did it at evening, so looking through my files I found a sunset which had been taken some years previously.

These two negatives were projected on to a film through the regular Montage method, (see chapter XIII) and then in turn this film positive was placed in the enlarger and projected on to a single weight paper which, of course, gave me the paper negative. This paper negative was in turn finally printed by contact on Opal Tapestry Z paper. Changes were made by retouching on both the positive and paper negative.

This gentleman is not only a man of the Cloth but he is a real man in every sense of the word—a great explorer, a scientist, and a vigorous outdoor type. When I took his picture I was impressed with the boldness of his profile, and while I know it was not the most flattering approach to reproducing his face, to me, the photographer, it was the most outstanding characteristic. At the time the picture was taken, Father Hubbard had just returned from one of his Alaskan expeditions, on which he had been presented with a marvelous cloak that had been hand-sewn by the Eskimos and had taken an enormous amount of labor. In order to show a bit more of the design of the cloak, it was considered best to photograph it from such an angle that it was necessary to pose him with his back towards the camera. Such a pose is ordinarily very dangerous when taking the average man, as it is usually more suitable to women. However, with the strong features of Father Hubbard I did not have to worry whether the picture would be masculine enough after being finished. When I take a photograph of a real, rugged individual I rarely resort to retouching, and in this case no retouching of any sort was done, although the image was slightly diffused during the enlarging in order to soften down some of the strong contrasts. The picture was printed on a 14 x 17 buff stock and slightly toned in selenium.

As a note of added interest, Father Hubbard has also served as a chaplain to our soldiers fighting in the Aleutians.

HELEN T. FARRELL

This study is in a low-key, by which we mean a picture where there, is a minimum of highlights and a maximum of shadows. Low-key is very effective where you wish to give a "Rembrant" touch to a portrait. It also seems to add mystery and gives more weight or seriousness to the study. It's especially helpful if we wish to dramatize a subject and can be very effective if we daringly lose the outline of the figure against the background. This picture was taken as a professional portrait of another photographer.

191

Photographing people is comparatively simple when we confine the picture to merely representing the head and shoulders. When it comes to making a three-quarter figure study, we have to be more careful as to focusing and lighting. I usually do not attempt to make three-quarter studies unless the subject seems to be adaptable to that type of posing. The picture of Miss Betty Furness was very simple to take because she, being a trained and graceful actress, fell into a pleasing position naturally and without strain.

I have always felt that when a photographer shows pictures of people connected either with the stage or movies, or pictures of professional models, that he should get very little credit for the actual job. Personally, I think it is almost ridiculously simple to take pleasing pictures of professionally trained and attractive people. I am a lot more inclined to give tremendous credit to the unsuspecting amateur who tries to take a glamour picture of poor Aunt Tillie.

This picture of Miss Furness would be classified as high-key because most of the tones are in the upper register. Of course, to get a picture of that type we must have a white background and the subject should be clothed in either white or pastel shades. While some are inclined to think high-key also means that the subject should have blonde hair, I have never been able to see the logic in such reasoning for the simple reason that high-key, in its real interpretation, is a two-line presentation instead of a third dimensional effort, and the best examples of two-line or notan art happen to be the Oriental form, or even the early Italian primitives, and I seem to recall very few blondes among those particular pictures. In other words high-key in its broader interpretation can be done with either blondes, brunettes or redheads.

LOUISE

The picture of Louise is the kind of informal portrait which we can take of our friends in the outdoors. Some of our most successful pictures may never sell or hang in an exhibition but they may make our hobby a more pleasant one by making our friends happier. Basically, this is a snapshot of a charming woman, but by arranging to have her face turned towards the light and by finding a convenient cherry tree, the whole setting becomes more attractive. Therefore, what might have been an ordinary snapshot becomes a very successful portrait of the subject. Taken with a 35 mm. camera.

FUTURE

This shot was taken on an assignment to Philadelphia. I had been told to go to Philadelphia and see what a New York photographer would find interesting in our neighboring city. Of course dozens of different types of pictures were taken but this particular one has always appealed to me because it seemed to be more "evident" than it would be in a city such as New York. By that I mean that there are any number of high buildings in New York where it would be possible to find a window washer hanging out, doing his daily chore, but somehow when I walked along in the good city of Philadelphia, the number of high buildings being less, this particular one caught my attention immediately. When I saw the window cleaner busy at work, the thought immediately struck me of what an endless task this job must be, starting in on Monday morning on a lower floor and working all week up to the higher floors, only to have to start over again next Monday—therefore, the title "Future." The picture was taken deliberately from a low viewpoint and at a steep angle in order to accentuate the height of the building. The building itself, while not particularly tall, seems to be much bigger because of the close cropping which gives the effect of an endless number of windows on all sides.

This is a sample of what a 35 mm. camera with a fast lens will be able to do where the larger camera would be a complete failure. It is an unposed picture taken of a man and his daughter, walking rapidly while actually being indoors. The picture was taken against the light coming in through a glass wall. The pattern of the windows makes an interesting design on the highly polished floors, and the whole combination, the moving feet, the repetition of the wall and floor design, give a good sense of rhythm. It was taken with a 35 mm. camera, shot at 1/125 of a second at *f2*. The picture was enlarged up to 16 x 20 on glossy paper. It is a straight print with the exception that the top and edges have been slightly darkened during enlarging.

THE RUSSIAN

The picture of the Russian may help you in your work—in two ways—first as to how to get certain subject material if you are interested in making character studies: One of my minor hobbies is research work in the culinary establishments in and around New York, which means visiting restaurants of all types and eating all sorts of strange foods. On one of these excursions I found my Russian giving a demonstration of knife throwing in a floor show. He immediately struck me as being a type that was genuinely Russian, one who should make an interesting picture. After his performance I approached the gentleman and he very readily agreed to come down to the studio and pose for a few pictures. And here's where we had a bit of fun, because I had noticed him from my table just as I had been reading about the Russian victories, and I imagined every Russian to be rather a stalwart, forceful, if not tough character— but in the studio upon closer acquaintance I found that my particular Russian, while he was stalwart enough, turned out to be a very pleasant, friendly chap who was anything but belligerent. As a matter of fact, in order to make him look more menacing I had to urge him to put on a tough expression and then later on with Farmer's Reducer I brightened up the whites of the eyes to emphasize this effect. What I mean to convey, is that quite often you can find inter-

esting people who will give you unusual pictures, but it may be necessary to do some improvising at the last minute, especially if they are not professional photographic models.

The second interesting item, which may prove to be a fruitful idea to you at times, is the fact that two pictures can quite often be made out of one negative. These two pictures are made from the same negative. In one, three-quarters of the figure is shown, which as stated elsewhere, is the most difficult portraiture or character work to do, and in the other the negative has been cropped to show merely the head and shoulders. That is the easiest kind of portraiture to do and you generally get the greatest amount of credit for it. Posing people for three-quarters or full length requires more thought as to lighting and also more care as to focusing, so that all planes will be approximately sharp. Merely taking a head and shoulders is a comparatively easy job and in addition to that, because of the greater "poster effect," (the carrying power of the larger image), you will very often receive more credit for that type of picture, especially from salon juries. Anyway, look through your negatives and see if there are not some which might perhaps be improved by further cropping.

DOWN TO THE SEA
(Pages 204-205)

In the original version of this picture the boat was traveling from left to right and, in this particular instance, it was felt that because the eye was traveling WITH the boat, it actually was led OUT of the picture without any feeling of emphasis.

So, paradoxically, by turning the picture around—still allowing the eye to travel normally from left to right—the mental impact is greater when the eye meets the ONCOMING boat. As mentioned elsewhere, many pictures can be improved by simply turning the negative around in the enlarger.

Also in the original picture, the upper sky was very light and distracted attention from the boat. It was a very simple matter to darken the upper areas down and to lighten up that portion of the sky which met the sails. In other words, the standard method of creating emphasis was utilized; that is, bringing the strongest highlights and strongest shadows together. To facilitate the work, the picture was made into a paper negative and printed by contact on 16 x 20 enlarging paper, then brown-toned to simulate the sunset.

GRAY DAWN

This picture was taken on a winter morning a few years back along the New York waterfront. A tug boat was maneuvering a barge toward the middle of the river, just as an ocean-going steamer slowly moved down the bay. I took the shot with a small vest pocket camera which I usually had in my coat during those days, but was a bit disappointed in the film's failure to record the fog.

In deciding to alter the picture, I made use of a paper negative, and desiring to obtain the greatest amount of grain and texture, made the original positive on a single weight paper. On this positive I sketched in a man who presumably was waving to a friend on the departing barge, who also had to be drawn in. Further, on this positive, I broke open the ice as though the barge had just left the position near the dock. This was all comparatively simple because it was being done on paper. Then from this positive a paper negative was made by contact. On the paper negative the smoke from the tug was made stronger and the picture was then printed on a slow enlarging paper and blue toned.

TWO LADIES

The negative of this picture is one of the most "perfect" in my collection. By perfect I mean more in the technical sense, as it has the long range of gradation, the perfect scale, and the brightness range representing the original scene. Of course, I deliberately picked the subject for that purpose, and I selected it at a time when there would be sunlight on it. Without sunlight it would have been practically impossible to get the long range of tones. We learn very quickly that if we want bright or brilliant pictures we must take them on bright or brilliant days. If you take a picture on a sunless, dull day you should, if you merely develop normally, not expect to have a bright, brilliant picture. I was first attracted by the **architectural setting** of this scene which is the well known spot on the corner of Fifth Avenue and 59th Street, and after walking around it a few times decided to take it from this particular angle where I could frame the picture with a tree. It also gave me an opportunity to get a few shadows in the foreground from the tree itself. The seated figure was deliberately posed in order to "balance" the statue itself. This is the kind of negative that when placed in a normal enlarger and printed on average No. 2 paper gives a perfect technical print without any manipulation or trouble of any sort—a very rare occasion indeed. In order, of course, to maintain good sharpness both in near and distant objects it was necessary to use a tripod, the exposure being approximately 1/10 of a second at $f18$. To bring out the perfect detail, texture, and long scale, the picture was printed on glossy paper and ferrotyped.

CONNECTICUT TREE

This interesting tree formation was found in the foot-hills of the Berkshires along a Connecticut road, at a time when the sky was simply hopeless. As you probably know, when the sky is a light gray or very pale blue, there is actually not much sense in using a filter, because unless a filter has a definite color in the sky to work upon, about the only result you get is a prolongation of your exposure. In such instances it is sometimes best merely to expose for the object you have in mind and to forget about the sky. As a matter of fact, if it blocks up, that is, if the sky becomes entirely opaque on the negative, you are sometimes better off because you will then find it easier to print in cloud combinations. In this instance I did not feel it necessary to add actual clouds as the composition of the tree itself was already quite intricate and the addition of clouds may only have made it more complicated. The only thing done in the printing was first to print the picture of the tree and then resort to "flashing" in order to darken the sky. The flashing was done on four sides of the print. The telegraph wires in the lower right hand corner were re-touched out with pencil directly on the 9 x 12 cm. negative, although if this had not been possible, a little more flashing in the area might have been sufficient to eliminate that objectionable feature.

VILLAGE ARTIST

Every year in New York we have an open air show where the independent artists have an opportunity to display their masterpieces and also make an extra penny sketching passersby.

This gentleman happened to be one of the artists who was making portraits of people on the spot, and when I spoke to him, he kindly stopped his work for a minute and allowed me to take a few pictures with my 35 mm. camera. Upon enlarging the picture I found that the background, an old door, seemed rather objectionable. Also I wanted to emphasize the portrait of the gentleman himself, and so resorted to the paper negative process.

I first made a positive on film, and on this transparency, with New Coccine, I darkened the area sufficiently so that the door disappeared. New Coccine also was used to darken the white shirt. I might recall to you that when New Coccine is used on a negative, it will *lighten* areas whereas if the dye is used on a positive, it will *darken* areas. This means, of course, that if we want to make a positive and from it another negative we have perfect control and can alter almost any values in the picture. By this positive-negative method we can turn light backgrounds into dark backgrounds and *vice versa* with comparative ease.

TREE BARK

As we all know, photography is a means of expressing yourself and telling the rest of the world what you see on this sphere. In a deeper sense everyone and everything we meet can be made into a picture, not perhaps a picture that everyone will like, for, as we have stated before, no picture has ever been made that everybody will like. If such a picture ever could be made, it would be a sorry state for all of us because it would be an indication that all our thoughts and lives had become so regimented that individual likes and dislikes had been eliminated entirely. The healthiest kind of an exhibition is one that displays many pictures you like, naturally, but there should be an actual number with which you violently disagree. That kind of a show, whether of photography or paintings, is helpful and stimulating and makes us think just a little more. This particular picture is a companion piece of "The Road Runs By." After all, they are both pictures of a tree. Naturally, to the average person who likes to find things represented in a sentimental and more or less conventional manner, "The Road Runs By" should have greater appeal.

210

To another individual whose mind is perhaps more analytical or who prefers things which have an abstract design or who loves a pattern, this entirely different interpretation of a tree may prove to be more interesting. It's all a question of viewpoint and of training. Personally, I like to keep my eyes open to almost every type of picture and I would very strongly suggest to the budding photographer that he should consider the world very much his own little oyster, one which should be thoroughly explored from all possible viewpoints and angles. This picture was made while taking out a group of students in Central Park on a very dull and dreary day.

Instead of taking a whole tree the camera was placed close to the bark in order to capture the pattern, and by twisting the camera sidewise, the pattern of the bark was made to run in a diagonal line to give it more of a dynamic touch. The actual absence of the sun, that is, working in a dull light, was extremely beneficial in getting full detail even in the deeper recesses of the bark. Inasmuch as this picture would be roughly classified as "modern" and as it depended upon its texture and definition, I carried out the full scheme by putting it on glossy paper, approximately 16 x 20 in size. To me, the picture of this bit of bark is just as intriguing as the more obvious pictorial shot of "The Road Runs By." While it may not have the emotional and sentimental appeal of a tree against the sky, it appeals more to the—if I may be permitted to say so—analytical side, which never is as popular, but at the same time is also important.

THE ROAD RUNS BY
(Page 214)

This picture has been extremely successful in exhibition work and therefore always reminds me that we can never be too dogmatic about laying down rules. For example, one of the best and most sensible rules to give to any aspiring photographer is to suggest that he confine the taking of his pictures to the hours before 10 in the morning and after 4 in the afternoon. In other words, try to coax him not to take his pictures during the middle noon hours of a summer's day, because at that time lighting is usually at its most uninteresting phase. This particular picture was taken about 12 o'clock noon and merely goes to prove that there are exceptions to any rule. So that the shot would get a little more of the quality called "pictorial" the picture was finally made into a paper negative and printed by contact on that most exquisite paper, Gevaluxe.

THE TUMULT

I deliberately tried to take this picture so that the whitest area of the rushing, tumbling stream would be contrasted against the darkest blacks. In order to further emphasize this, the edges and corners of the picture were, of course, printed darker. This picture was taken hand-held with a 3¼ x 4¼ camera and was shot at approximately 1/100 of a second at *f*8. I have read many statements suggesting that in order to give realism to rushing or falling water we should use comparatively slow shutter speeds so as not to "freeze" the action of the water itself. I personally have never been converted to that method of taking fast moving water because I have seen too many pictures, taken with comparatively slow shutter speeds, in which the water looked a lot more artificial than it would had it been taken with faster action. Always, when I use a *small* camera to photograph rushing water I like to use a speed of 1/200 or even 1/400 of a second, because I keep trying to remember that my 35 mm. or 2¼ square negative may have to be enlarged anywhere from 8 to 15 or more diameters, which, of course, means that unless I have taken the onrushing waves or waterfall at a high speed, the picture will completely fall apart when it is enlarged.

This picture is one of those taken on the spur of the moment and had to be taken under the worst possible conditions—it had to be taken quickly or not at all. I happened to be walking near Radio City when I was attracted to the sky by passersby. It was already too late to see the airplane which had made the sky writing, but the lettering was still drifting lazily into the summer sun. I realized I had an opportunity to take a picture with a different slant. Placing the camera on the ground and stopping it well down I maneuvered in such a way that I had a traffic sign in front of my lens. By merely exposing for the sky, the traffic signal became practically a silhouette. Printed in a natural manner the picture is rather uninteresting as the lower portion appears lighter because that is the way nature shows it to us. Being intent upon dramatizing the picture, I maintained a fairly white area during the printing with a dodger, which I kept moving right near where the traffic sign is placed. The traffic signal itself, being practically a silhouette and very transparent on the negative, did not show any evidence of having the blacks held back. Then to finish the picture a thorough job of flashing was done on all four sides and corners of the print. This is, therefore, a print made from one negative in which deliberate over-dodging was done in the center, with strong flashing on all sides, including the bottom.

REVERIE

This study of a young lady was originally taken against a dark background and was not intended to be a high key, but by the proper manipulation of New Coccine, the shadows of the face were sufficiently lightened up to become very faint and the background was made to appear light. The oval effect was added later on, merely as a matter of experiment, as I felt that the picture seemed to be more graceful in that type of frame than in the conventional rectangular shape. I fully realize that, to many people, the oval shape seems a bit old-fashioned but here, too, I believe the individual should use his own judgment and do exactly as he pleases. Further than that, the picture was made up in two different colors—one was made in a red chalk and one was blue-toned, and somehow I have always personally preferred the blue-toned even though the red chalk is a standardized method of handling this sort of study.

"Winter Morn" was taken about 10 minutes after "Gray Dawn" (page 203) with the same simple, small camera. I took many a picture with this camera which I had picked up in a store for about $8.00. While the lens itself was not too good, it was a genuine vest pocket affair so that it could be comfortably carried without bulking one's clothing. However, I soon found that when the pictures were enlarged to any real size the camera lens did not have good enough definition to produce the sharpness and detail we expect in a straight enlargement. I, therefore, found it very convenient to resort to the paper negative process for pictures taken with this camera. While the paper negative method may not be in tremendous favor in the commercial world, it does give the amateur a great opportunity to alter his pictures and have lots of fun, to say the least. I have always maintained that if I had only a box Brownie or a similar inexpensive camera, and I was desirous of getting into the exhibition game, I would use the paper negative process for most of my pictures. When you come down to it, once you make a paper negative, it makes little difference whether you took the picture with a $500 camera or with a $2.00 camera. Here the sky was considerably dramatized, the foreground altered and in a general sense the whole picture changed from its original appearance.

THE GHOST TREE

While wandering through the Jersey countryside with a student, we came across this old and deserted house which at one time must have been part of a lovely and prosperous farm. The surrounding vegetation had been allowed to overgrow and the interior of the house had become very much dilapidated. It made one feel a bit sad to think of what had been, and wandering about the place in that mood I was struck by the shadow of a tree on one side of the house. As the wind was blowing rather strongly at the time, the noise of the swishing leaves, combined with the eerie surroundings, made one think of ghosts. Of course later on, returning to the city and making up the print in the darkroom, much of the effect felt at the time of taking the picture was missing because the noise of the rushing wind was gone and the moving tree had been so taken that the leaves would

not be blurry, and now the picture was more or less of a static affair. The picture had been taken on a summer's day with a good bright sun and the thought occurred to me that if, instead of printing it as a positive I showed it as a negative, a closer approach could be maintained to the original conception. In order to print the picture as a negative on paper it was necessary to make a positive on film. This was very easily accomplished, of course, by taking the original negative and printing it in contact with a commercial film, which gave me the positive. This positive was then placed in the enlarger and projected in the same manner as when making a regular print. The picture was taken with a 2¼ x 2¼ reflex camera. In order to show the contrast and perhaps to suggest to you similar ideas, we are showing here both the print as it actually looked when printed from the regular negative and the picture as printed from the positive.

THE OUTCAST

In many cases "run of the mill" pictures can, with a bit of imagination, be altered to be interesting and definitely dramatic. Often we find that a man who is technically proficient in his work

is apt to be a bit less imaginative when he starts making his prints in the darkroom. Don't be afraid to try for new and unusual effects. Don't hesitate to change the tone values. YOU should be the judge whether you want your pictures lighter or darker. If "The Outcast" had been printed as the scene actually appeared, it would not leave much of an impression. However, by deliberately over-printing ninety per cent of the picture and by holding back the balance near the center with a small dodger, we get an eerie effect. The only bright spot now remaining is a bit of sky along the upper edge of the deserted barge. The final picture has no more resemblance to the original than day has to night—but when we are making pictures to please *ourselves,* that in itself is of very little importance. The trick, of course, is to know where to print in and where to hold back. Inasmuch as the eye will always be attracted quickest to the spot where the strongest highlights and strongest shadows meet, I deliberately made the clouds lighter near the sharp angle of the old derelict by dodging, thus improving the composition and emphasizing a center of interest.

"Sand Hog" is not submitted as being one of the finest pictures ever made but merely as another illustration that through the medium of printing technique we can greatly improve what might ordinarily be a hopeless case, from the photographic standpoint. The original was taken on a flatly lighted, Sunday morning, when I ran into this gentleman just as he was preparing to go down into the bowels of Mother Earth to do his part in constructing the tunnel under the East River. I coaxed him to give me at least one shot of him and then I did the rest in the darkroom. First I turned the negative completely around in order to change the composition. Reversing the negative thusly, in practically one-third of all cases, will give better composition to many pictures. When you make a proof, always be sure to check whether an improvement can be gained by following this simple procedure. Of course, you must remember when you do this in an enlarger, in order to maintain sharpness of the image, you must re-focus the negative because the emulsion side is not at the same distance from the lens as before. After the negative was turned around, the only other thing done to make the picture more impressive, was to add a vigorous job of flashing so that light was concentrated around the head itself, all other portions of the picture being subordinated.

THE NIGHT RAID

From a record shot of a small road sign, with a 35mm. camera, this picture was made into an interesting print by cropping out unwanted sections and deliberately over-printing the sky to give the effect of a night scene. Dodging was used to lighten some areas with final touches being put in with Farmer's reducer. The print was toned to a rather warm, reddish tint which gives the effect of a glowing, burning sky.

CHAPTER XVIII

CHOOSING THE PAPER FOR YOUR SUBJECT MATTER

O NE of the questions most often asked is: which paper should I use for a portrait?—or which paper should I use for a land-scape?—or in fact the basic question is—what paper is proper for any particular subject? Whenever you are in doubt, or whenever you cannot make up your mind, remember that you will always be in good taste and not get into any trouble by choosing first of all a white paper stock. A plain white stock in its essential sense is suitable to all photographic printing purposes regardless of the subject matter. It will prove equally inoffensive to the layman, to the professional, and to the salon judge, and it is, therefore, always "safe." When it comes to choosing the best all-round paper surface, I would suggest that a fairly smooth luster surface would also be the safest all-round bet. In other words, if you were limited to choosing only one paper and you were going to be called upon to do all types of pictures from portraits to landscapes, to commercial, professional, and documen-tary work, the best all-round paper would be a smooth luster surface on a white stock.

GLOSSY PAPER

However, and fortunately, the manufacturers have kindly pro-vided us with many surfaces and many colored stocks of paper so we can escape monotony. For example, the pictures which I make for reproduction purposes are usually made on a glossy paper and preferably ferrotyped. If you are a technician who desires to prove that photography has the greatest capacity of any graphic medium for rendering shades and subtle nuances of lights and tones, there

Papers	Negative Required with Brand of Paper	Characteristics
BROMIDES		High Printing Spee
Brovira	Less Brilliant	Lend themselves contrast varia' through changes ir veloper.
Dassonville	Very Brilliant	
P.M.C.	Brilliant	
Press Bromide	Less Brilliant	
FAST CHLORO-BROMIDES		Medium Printing S
Cykora	Fairly Brilliant	Lend themselves contrast varia' through changes in veloper.
Halobrome	Less Brilliant	
Kodabromide	Brilliant	
Velour Black	Less Brilliant	
SLOW CHLORO-BROMIDES		Slow Printing Spee
Illustrators' Special	Brilliant	Difficult to change trast by developer iation only.
Indiatone	Brilliant	
Kodalure	Brilliant	
Projecto	Brilliant	
Veltura	Brilliant	
Vitava Opal	Brilliant	

GENERAL NOTES: A good tip-off on the characteristics of a paper is a ch and white work but not suitable for direct toning and sponds to tone changes by development, the warmer i quire more brilliant negatives. All papers look best wh

*The above table is based on the "Normal" of each paper stock, white base. C

HEIR CHARACTERISTICS

Image Tone	Toning	Remarks
Blue-black		
tone secured with -Q or Amidol de-er.	Not recommended except for sepia-bleach and re-development process.	#4 Brovira usually most contrasty of all enlarging papers.
blackish to warm ish.		
tone secured with -Q or Amidol de-er.	Sepia bleach and re-development, Hypo alum toner. May be toned with "direct" toner but do not react to selenium and gold chloride toners as well as slow chloro-bromides.	Most popular type of papers in use today. Best for beginner to standardize upon and most widely used by professionals in enlarging.
Variation Pos-in tone.		Slow chloro-bromides are available in one contrast grade only—negative must be made to fit paper.
ugh change in de-er or change in de-ng time. All sorts des of warm black dish tone possible "warm" tone de-rs.	Excellent results obtainable with selenium type toners and gold chloride blue toners. **Excellent for portraiture and pictorial work.**	Kodalure has warmest (brownish) tone of all papers without toning. Emulsion is easily damaged by rough handling.

ed. In almost all cases a fast paper will give cold black tones—good for black
d with warm tone developers. The slower the paper the more readily it re-
e better the results obtained with direct toning. The slow papers usually re-
they dry down darker—especially matte and semi-matte stock.

k, grade, etc., will modify these comments.

is no better proof in the world than a print on glossy paper which has been competently ferrotyped. It will give you your most brilliant highlights, detailed middle tones and end up with the strongest, richest blacks. Technically, there is no argument about that. Artistically, however, many people feel that a glossy paper looks a bit too "commercial," but that, too, is a matter of opinion, as some of the finest exhibition pictures ever made were put on glossy paper. There is only one catch to the use of a glossy paper and that perhaps is the greatest single factor why it has never become as popular with the amateur as with the professional, and that is, you must have a practically perfect negative to be able to use the paper to its full effectiveness. A glossy paper not only shows the greatest and longest gradations but is also the best paper for showing minute detail and that is why so many of the smaller prints are always delivered ferrotyped on glossy paper. But, if it has the ability to show minute details it can also very decidedly show faults in the negative better than any other type of paper. Grain, dust, pinholes, etc., all become exaggerated on glossy paper.

Another thing about glossy paper, no matter what the color of the print may be, whether black, brown, blue, or green, or whatever you may choose to make it, it will be the most brilliant color possible and no other surface will be able to equal it.

HANDLE GLOSSY PAPER CAREFULLY

The surface of a glossy paper is very easily damaged when carelessly handled. This is not often realized by those who first attempt to use glossy paper, but when handling it in the developer, fixer, and washing, especially when large prints such as 14 x 17 or 16 x 20 are made, the paper must always be handled with two hands and always turned in such a way that there is no sudden jerk or quick folding over, or the emulsion will be cracked after the drying. While the glossy paper is practically the standby in professional work, it has never quite assumed equal popularity among exhibitors, although previous to the war quite a bit of excitement was caused in American exhibitions by the success of Czechoslovakian and Hungarian workers who, in the late '30s, insisted on using practically nothing else but glossy papers for even their most misty atmospheric effects. There is one thing about a glossy picture—when it stands on the exhibition board and the jury sits 6 or 7, or even 8 or 10 feet away, it will usually pop out at them with greater emphasis than any other type of print. One big advantage glossy paper has to offer the average worker is that it is about the only paper which will dry down to about the same depth and brilliance as it seemed to have while it was still wet in the washing tray. All other surfaces, as we know from sad experience, dry down much duller and quite often to such an extent that they do not seem to be the same print we made the night previously.

You will usually find glossy paper most suitable for industrial scenes, for pictures where great clarity and brilliance is most essential, and, of course, where detail must be shown in its most minute form. A good example of the use of glossy paper to the best advantage may be seen from "Texture," on page 181, where it helps to bring out the texture and detail of the cloth better than any other paper.

PORTRAIT PAPERS

When I make portraits, I usually prefer to put them on a buff stock and a warm tone paper—that means any of the slow chlorobromide papers will be very suitable. The reason I like to print my portraits in a warm tone is that I am trying to give an imitation surface appearance of the subject himself. When we look at a face we notice, among the strongest colors, shades of yellow, burnt sienna, brown, and even pink. Generally speaking, therefore, faces of healthy people have a warm color. Therefore, by using a buff stock or even a warm tone stock we come closer to the actual appearance of the individual. Just as we seem to glow a bit more after a healthy tan, the picture with the warm color seems to do the same thing for us. I rarely would sell a cold looking print to any customer, and when it comes to exhibition work I may even go further—after a print has been printed on the warm tone paper I may additionally tone it in a selenium or Nelson toner giving an extra brownish cast to the whole print. Here, too, the warm tone developers such as Glycin or Adurol are very useful to get brown tones.

ELIMINATING A YELLOWISH CAST

This extra toning is especially adaptable if the original tone of the print, by direct development, has a slightly yellowish cast. In such a case sometimes a slight toning of 4 or 5 seconds may be sufficient to eliminate the yellow cast. It will not be necessary to warn you that when you tone a print it is always advisable to have previously thoroughly soaked it in plain water for 5 minutes so that any toning action will take place evenly all over the print, which will not be the case if a dry print is suddenly immersed into a quick-working toner.

The buff or the warm tone print is also extremely popular when used for pictorial effects, especially where we wish to get a feeling of sunshine, or for beach scenes where lots of sand is present. Other instances would be the use of a warm tone or buff stock for sunsets, or in conjunction with printing from paper negatives or other manipulated printing processes where the straight photographic medium seems to have been tampered with. A warm tone print also seems to have a greater sentimental value and, therefore, is popular with many people because it appeals to their emotional sense. The straight white stock could be said to appeal more to the abstract or intellectual type, and, of course, that type of person is always in the minority. Salon exhibitors who either have sensed that or who merely make pictures which appeal to their own instincts quite often lean toward the warm tone prints because of this sentimental and emotional value.

Blue-toning is usually best on white stock and it is most suitable for snow scenes. It is also valuable for pictures where a brilliant sky takes up the greatest amount of area, whether it would be a landscape or a seascape. While blue toning can be done on papers with a buff stock, in such instances it is best confined to pictures where you wish to give a certain mysterious effect, as in night scenes or early morning landscapes. However, whenever in doubt about blue toning, stick to the white stock for marines and night scenes. But if you are merely out to please yourself, you can, of course, use that particular effect for any picture that you wish. Years ago Reynolds painted the famous Blue Boy and by doing so caused quite a bit of art controversy, and there is no reason why you too cannot also tone a picture of a person in a blue tone if you so feel inclined, especially if you do not have to please any judges in exhibitions. For example, I myself felt that if Reynolds could make a blue boy, I could make a blue girl. The original print of the picture "Orientale" on page 134, has always been shown as a blue toned, high-key print, and the judges have been very kind to it in letting it pass through for hanging.

CHAPTER XIX

BLUE AND BROWN TONING

BLUE TONING

PROBABLY the photographic process most frequently admired by amateurs is that which gives brilliant blue or blue-black tones. While there are many methods by which papers can be blue-toned, there is no better way than by using the gold chloride solution to get the best effect. The gold chloride works in direct ratio to the amount of silver in the print. That is, wherever there is no metallic silver in the print, such as in the margins or in the clear highlights of the picture, the gold chloride will not have any effect on the paper, but will simply confine its work to the areas in which we have some silver present, such as in the middle tones and blacks. Other blue-toners quite often achieve their results by "dyeing" the whole print, giving a final appearance of fogged bluish highlights—which usually means that the print is a complete failure. To get the best results in gold chloride blue toning you should keep in mind some of the following:

First:—Everything being equal, the most brilliant blue tones will be secured on glossy papers, the dullest blue tones on matte papers. Sometimes a paper which dries down too dull can be made to appear more brilliant by varnishing or waxing, after the print has dried, this giving an added luster to the print. But make sure the wax or varnish is not too yellowish.

Second:—Papers of the slow chloro-bromide variety will always be more successful for blue toning than papers of the fast chloro-bromide type. That means a paper such as Kodalure or Veltura will give a much finer result than fast papers such as Kodabromide or Velour Black, although unquestionably all these papers can be used for blue toning. When you run into a real bromide paper such as PMC or Brovira, blue toning through the use of gold-chloride will prove rather futile, although I have sometimes used the blue toning formula on such fast bromide papers for a half hour or so, in order to eliminate a brownish tone and to secure a more pleasing blue-black tone.

Third:—Regardless of the paper used, if you have developed in Adurol, Glycin, or Pyrocatechin, you will secure a lighter bluish tone; or, in other words, any developer which by direct development will give a print a brownish color will make that print very adaptable for blue toning.

Fourth:—It is advisable to use a plain FRESH hypo for fixing, or at most an acid hypo. By using only fresh hypo you will eliminate many troubles at the outset. If you use a hypo which contains a hardener such as alum, you will find it very difficult, although not altogether impossible, to get real, strong, blue tones. Of course, the blue toner solution has a tendency to soften the emulsion of the paper during toning, especially the Kodalure emulsion. In such instances you can tone the print, give it a short 2 or 3 minute rinse in plain water, and then re-harden it in the Formalin hardener (page 253) or a hardener-hypo, such as the F-5 (page 252).

In any other cases where you find upon touching the emulsion, that it has considerably softened up after blue toning, it might be advisable to reharden the print or, at least after washing, to let it first dry by hanging it up without allowing the emulsion to touch any blotter or any other surface. If the emulsion has been excessively softened and you lay the print down to dry, you may be embarrassed the next day to find that it has stuck to the surface with which you put it in contact.

Fifth:—Another factor which influences the brilliance of blue toning is the strength of your gold chloride solution. If you wish to splurge a bit (or if you expect a legacy soon) you can always use the formula 3 or 4 times stronger than suggested—that is, instead of taking the usual 1 ounce out of each of the 3 bottles plus 10 ounces of water, (see formula, page 250) you can simply add only 3 or 4 ounces of water. That, of course, means that you will have to use up a lot more of the gold chloride solution in order to cover a 14 x 17 or 16 x 20 exhibition print. When you remember that gold chloride is a rather expensive item, costing approximately $1.35 to $1.50 for 15 grains, you will have to decide personally to what extent you wish to go in this direction.

Sixth:—Another thing which will rather help toward the securing of the bluish tones is the temperature of the toning solution. Normally the temperature should be 65° to 70°F. when in use but in some obstinate cases when the action seems sluggish you may secure a very successful result by heating up the formula to 75°, 80°, or even 90°F. One word of caution, however—do not try this on a paper such as Kodalure which has a very beautiful but extremely sensitive emulsion, or you may find the gelatin softening to the extent that it leaves the paper forever.

The above hints should take the mystery out of blue toning. In addition to that, it is just as well to be wise and avoid the use of contrasty papers in blue toning because papers of the No. 3 and No. 4 grades are either impossible or extremely difficult to blue tone successfully. Also, papers intended for blue toning should be even more thoroughly washed than average prints. If any appreciable hypo remains in the print when you start the blue toning, one of two things will result—you will either get a very nasty yellow-brown stain, or the blue toning will take an inordinately long time and then will not be very good. Also, the gold chloride will wear out much quicker. Usually when I wash prints for blue toning, I wash them for a minimum of 2 hours and see to it that they are quite often turned around. Every 15 to 20 minutes the bottom prints are placed on top and vice-versa, and the prints are usually washed emulsion downwards, giving a chance for all of the hypo to wash out. This is especially important during the wintertime when, if the water temperature is low, it may then be a good idea to wash them first in a controlled water temperature of 65° to 70° for 15 to 20 minutes, even if you have to stay with them in order to see that the temperature remains constant. In such a way you can eliminate most of the hypo and then the balance of the washing can be done in the lower temperature of the cold tap water.

To sum up, to get the best results on blue toning: (1) Use a paper with a brilliant surface. (2) Use one of the slower emulsions

237

such as Veltura or Kodalure. (3) Use a slow developer which gives a direct brown tone, such as Adurol or Glycin. (4) Do not use any hardener. (5) Thoroughly wash all hypo from print before toning.

If everything works all right, it usually will take from 10 minutes to 30 minutes to get a perfect blue tone. How long it actually does take will depend upon the depth of the silver content in your print, that is, a high-key print with very few blacks in it will tone easier and more readily than a low-key print which has very strong blacks in it. For example, a picture such as "Dedication" (frontispiece) not only takes a longer time to blue tone but also exhausts the gold chloride solution more quickly because there is such a large amount of silver in the blacks which have to be converted, whereas a print such as "Orientale" on page 134 which is in a high key and therefore has proportionately a very small amount of real black area will tone very quickly and the gold chloride solution will be able to tone 3 or 4 prints before becoming exhausted, as compared to only one print of the "Dedication" type.

One thing to remember in blue toning is that usually a print will be *intensified* after the toning. A print which dries down just right may unfortunately be slightly too dark when you are through with blue toning, whereas a print which is slightly too weak may be just of the right quality after the toning. This is because the gold chloride, as stated previously, works on the silver content of the print—it adds to and plates the silver deposit but does not add anything to the highlights, the noticeable result being that the print seems to have been made more contrasty. However, after one or two trials you will be able to determine just how strong your print should be *before* blue toning. If you have any doubt about it simply make a good print, as usual, but just slightly less contrasty, but be sure the highlights of the print are kept clear and white.

BROWN TONING

Personally when I desire brownish tones, I go about it the easiest way by selecting the types of papers which are very susceptible to giving warm tones either through direct development or direct toning. Except in special cases, I do not try to get brown tones by the bleach and re-development method.

If you wish to get warm tones you should use the slow chlorobromides such as Kodalure, Opal, Veltura, Indiatone or papers of

238

similar type. If you do not use too much carbonate in your developer, you will find it exceedingly easy to get pleasing warm tones merely by ordinary methods of development. Of course, if you use the developer with an excessive amount of carbonate, the tones will tend to go toward the cold blacks.

After washing, if the warmth of tone obtained is not as strong as you desire, it is then very easy to get a warmer tone by transferring the print to a direct toner such as one of the selenium type which can be purchased ready for use, at your dealer. Any of the slow chloro-bromides and many of the fast chloro-bromides will tone very handsomely in a direct toner of this type and without trouble.

Of one thing you must be sure—that before you transfer your prints to this direct toner they should have been fixed in FRESH hypo and washed very thoroughly, and it may even be preferable to let them dry. Letting them dry first will not only give you an opportunity to study the exact color, but will also enable the gelatin to become toughened up before being subjected to a secondary process.

The great advantage of the direct toning system is that you can watch the print and stop the action at any moment by simply transferring the picture to a tray of running water. If later on you find that you stopped the toning too quickly, there is nothing to prevent you from again immersing the print into the toner a day, a week, or even a month later and continue toward a browner or redder image.

Naturally, not all papers react in the same manner to these toners. For example, a paper such as Kodalure can be toned to a very warm brown in four to five seconds' time if the toner is fresh or if the temperature is too high, while other prints of the faster chloro-bromide types such as Kodabromide may take anywhere from 10 minutes to one hour in the solution before you get the desired effect. In case you are not too familiar with brands of paper, save unwanted prints and take an evening off and test them in the toner to see how each one reacts. Through this method you will gain valuable judgment as to reactions of papers to the toner. However, if you are using straight bromide papers, about the only satisfactory and safe way in which to get brown or sepia prints is to resort to the old method of bleaching and re-development.

CHAPTER XX

FORMULARY

DEVELOPERS FOR WARM TONES

Developers for brownish or "copper effects" by direct development. Most successful on Kodalure, Opal, Indiatone, Veltura and "slow" papers.

ADUROL DEVELOPER

Adurol is one of the finest all-around developing agents for producing brownish prints by direct development. It may also be used for negative development but not for miniature work. "Adurol" is a foreign trade name for the monochloride substitute for hydroquinone. In this country it has been put out under various names and with various degrees of reliability. It is obtainable from most dealers under the names—Chlornol, Chlor-Quinon, etc. It is a great boon to those who suffer from Metol poisoning as it does not attack the skin. Here is a good all-around formula:

	Avoirdupois	Metric
Water	*32 ounces*	*1.0 liter*
Adurol	*75 grains*	*5.1 grams*
Sodium sulphite	*300 grains*	*20.4 grams*
Sodium carbonate	*300 grains*	*20.4 grams*
Potassium bromide	*10 grains*	*0.7 grams*

Mix chemicals in order given.

Use full strength for ordinary tones on average papers and develop for about 2 minutes at 70° F. If you wish more brownish or reddish results, add 10, 20 or even 40 ounces (315, 625 or 1250 cc's) of water, then take a piece of your favorite paper and give it an over-exposure in the enlarger so that the image will come up in not less than 10 to 15 seconds.

However, before you start development, cut the paper in four equal pieces and immerse them all at the same time. After half-minute of development take out one of the pieces, after one minute remove the next piece, at one and one-half minutes remove the third and allow the last to remain until two minutes have elapsed.

Each one of these pieces will have a different shade of brown The shorter the development time, the browner the tone, the longer the development time, the colder the tone. These strips will give you an idea of what to expect when the print is immersed in the developer, and you can thus pre-determine the tone you prefer. This is very important in case you plan to blue tone the print later. If a light blue tone is desired from the gold chloride toner, the print should be developed on the short side as a brownish print will give the most brilliant blue in the toner.

Hydroquinone

Various beautiful color effects can be secured by adding Hydroquinone to the above developer. The amount should be about equal to that of the Adurol (75 grains) and should be dissolved after the Adurol and Sulphite.

FOR THE ADVANCED WORKER

The above Adurol formula does not have to be taken too literally by the advanced worker. Simply remember that if you increase the amount of Adurol, the developer will be stronger and more contrasty. Also, the less Sodium carbonate you use, the warmer the tone of the print. The use of too little carbonate, however, will result in a flat, muddy print.

You can experiment further by making up a stronger concentration and increase the amount of Potassium bromide to 40 or even 80 grains! Then, you should preferably add some old Metol-Hydroquinone developer. Expose the print so that development is finished within a minute, or at the most, a minute and a half. The longer the development is continued, the "quicker" the color disappears. By using a *concentrated* developer on the slow papers, such as Kodalure, even in the shortened development, you will overcome any tendency toward

241

flatness. This odd mixture of Adurol and Metol-Hydroquinone will serve to standardize the color of the prints if several have to be made from the same negative. To top it off, you can later, still further tone the print in a toner such as selenium.

Using Potassium Carbonate instead of Sodium Carbonate

The use of Potassium carbonate in place of Sodium carbonate will help greatly in obtaining warm tones by direct development. While Sodium carbonate is the standard alkali used in most developers, many advanced workers prefer to use the Potassium carbonate as it will give browner tones and because it can be used in stronger concentrations.

Pyrocatechin

This is also an interesting developing agent for use with paper. It is a slow working chemical and is practically interchangeable with Adurol. If you wish, you can substitute it in the Adurol formula given above.

Interesting effects can be obtained when mixed 50-50 with Hydroquinone or if mixed with a standard Metol-Hydroquinone formula but it will lose some of its warm tone when used this way. When correctly handled it will produce fascinating "copper" tones, which are suitable for either portraiture or pictorial landscapes.

EDWAL 106

AUTO-TONING DEVELOPER

(Courtesy of "Modern Developing Methods")

STOCK SOLUTION	Avoirdupois	Metric
Water	35 ounces	1 liter
Sulphite	3 ounces	85 grams
Sodium carbonate (Anhyd.)	5 ounces	145 grams
Monazol	1 ounce	28 grams
Hydroquinone	135 grains	9 grams
Potassium bromide	62 grains	4 grams

(Monazol is the Edwal brand of Glycin)

242

With contact paper, Edwal-106 produces tones that vary from greenish brown to sepia and brick-red. With slow chloro-bromide papers it produces delicate tones that are very beautiful in high-key work, and with the fast chloro-bromides it produces warm blacks and brown blacks.

For bromide papers, dilute with 3 parts of water for warm black tones. With Brovira, diluting Edwal-106 stock solution with 7 parts of water will produce brown tones. For chloride and chloro-bromide papers, dilute with 7 parts of water and develop for from 4 to 6 minutes for brown blacks. At a dilution of 15 to 1, Edwal-106 produces the so-called "Gravure-brown" tones on enlarging papers and delicate green and red tones on Opal and Tuma Gas, respectively.

When a large number of prints are to be made from one negative, the exact exposure and developing time necessary to produce the desired tone should be determined and then each print should be exposed and developed according to these times. Otherwise, it is sometimes hard to match tones exactly if development by inspection is relied upon.

Kodak D-52

For Warm Tone Papers

STOCK SOLUTION	Avoirdupois		Metric	
Water, about 125°F. (50°C.)	16	ounces	500	cc.
Elon (Metol)	22	grains	1.5	grams
Sodium sulphite				
(desiccated)	¾	ounce	22.5	grams
Hydroquinone	90	grains	6.3	grams
Sodium carbonate				
(desiccated)	½	ounce	15.0	grams
Potassium bromide	22	grains	1.5	grams
Cold water to make	32	ounces	1.0	liter

Dissolve chemicals in the order given.

For use, take 1 part stock solution to 1 part water. Develop not less than 1½ minutes at 70° F.

Note:—More bromide may be added if warmer tones are desired.

243

Ansco 135
Warm Tone Developer

STOCK SOLUTION	Avoirdupois	Metric
Hot water (125°F. or 52°C.)	24 ounces	750 cc.
Metol	24 grains	1.6 grams
Sodium sulphite,		
anhydrous ....¾ oz.	20 grains	24 grams
Hydroquinone	96 grains	6.6 grams
Sodium carbonate,		
monohydrated ....¾ oz.	20 grains	24 grams
Potassium bromide	40 grains	2.8 grams
Water to make	32 ounces	1.0 liter

For use, dilute 1 part stock solution with 1 part water. A properly exposed print will be fully developed at 70° F. (21° C.) in about 1½ to 2 minutes. Complete development may be expected to take slightly longer with rough surfaced papers than with semi-glossy or luster surfaced papers. For greater softness, dilute the bath with water up to equal quantities of developer and water. To increase the warmth add bromide up to double the amount in the formula. The quantity of bromide specified in the formula, however, assures rich, warm, well-balanced tones.

GENERAL PURPOSE DEVELOPERS
Ansco 125
Metol-Hydroquinone Developer

STOCK SOLUTION	Avoirdupois	Metric
Hot water (125°F. or 52°C.)	24 ounces	750 cc.
Metol	45 grains	3 grams
Sodium sulphite,		
anhydrous	1½ ounces	44 grams
Hydroquinone ....¼ oz.	60 grains	12 grams
Sodium carbonate,		
monohydrated	2¼ ounces	65 grams
Potassium bromide	30 grains	2 grams
Water to make	32 ounces	1 liter

Recommended for the development of Cykon, Cykora, Brovira and similar papers. It can also be used for the development of press films.

Paper Development: Dilute 1 part stock solution with 2 parts water. Develop 1 to 2 minutes at 70° F. (21° C.). For softer and slower development dilute 1 to 4 and develop 1½ to 3 minutes at 70° F. (21° C.). For greater brilliance, shorten the exposure slightly and lengthen the development time. For greater softness, lengthen exposure slightly and shorten development.

Film Development: Dilute 1 part stock solution with 3 parts water. Normal development time, Ansco press film 3 to 4 minutes at 65° F. (18° C.).

KODAK D-72
FOR PAPERS, FILMS, PLATES

STOCK SOLUTION	Avoirdupois	Metric
Water, about 125°F. (50°C.)	16 ounces	500 cc.
Elon (Metol)	45 grains	3.1 grams
Sodium sulphite		
(desiccated)	1½ ounces	45.0 grams
Hydroquinone	175 grains	12.0 grams
Sodium carbonate		
(desiccated)	2¼ ounces	67.5 grams
Potassium bromide	27 grains	1.9 grams
Water to make	32 ounces	1.0 liter

Dissolve chemicals in the order given.

For papers dilute 1 to 2 and develop about 45 seconds at 70° F. For films and plates, dilute 1 to 2 and develop about 4 minutes in a tray or 5 minutes in a tank at 65° F.

DEFENDER 55-D

STOCK SOLUTION	Avoirdupois	Metric
Water	32 ounces	1.0 liter
Metol	36 grains	2.4 grams
Sodium sulphite		
(Anhydrous)	1¼ ounces	36.0 grams
Hydroquinone	144 grains	10.0 grams
Sodium carbonate		
(Anhydrous)	1¼ ounces	36.0 grams
(or Monohydrated) ..1 oz. 204 grains		42.1 grams
Potassium bromide ......60–144 grains		4–13 grams

Mix in order given.

For use take 1 part above working solution and add 2 parts water.

The liberal use of Potassium bromide is strongly recommended, even in excess of quantity given above.

Bromide tends to slow up development, an advantage when working with a fast paper. It gives warm tones in Black and Sepia, assures rich luminous shadows and clear highlights, and builds up a soft print of true portrait quality.

Prints should be timed so as to develop in from 1½ to 2 minutes. The short development makes for warm tones, the longer development for cold tones.

Note: While manufacturer's instructions call for various development times I usually expose my prints so they will develop for 2 minutes, as explained in previous chapters. I deviate from the "2 minute" procedure only in special cases.

AMIDOL DEVELOPER

This Amidol developer formula gives real blacks with a fine scale and transparency in the shadows. Make up fresh.

	Avoirdupois	Metric
Water	32 ounces	1.0 liter
Sodium sulphite	360 grains	24.5 grams
Citric Acid	8 grains	0.6 grams
Amidol	120 grains	8.1 grams
Potassium bromide	8 grains	0.6 grams
Sulphocyanate	4 grains	0.3 grams

Mix in the order given.

For use, take full strength solution. Develop from 1½ minutes to 4 minutes at 70° F. For average results try first the "2 minute period" mentioned in preceding chapters. On a straight chloride paper a 3 minute period is usually very successful.

The addition of the Citric acid prevents stains on the paper.

The Sulphocyanate is not necessary, but it gives better blacks and has often been added to other developers to get truer black tones. Its use is recommended. Sodium thiocyanate may be substituted if Sulphocyanate cannot be had.

246

Brown Toning for Chloro-Bromide Papers

My favorite brown toners are the direct selenium toners, such as are sold by a number of firms. Of these, I especially like the Eastman and the Tuma toner, which give practically the same results. They work best on the slow chloro-bromide papers.

In using these, the print is first developed in the regular manner, fixed, washed and dried. It is then re-soaked in plain water for about 5 minutes and placed in the selenium toner. While in the solution it should be rocked continuously.

The toner will first turn the print to a warm black, then to a warm brown and, if left in the solution very long, to a reddish brown. How long the print should be left in the toner is up to the individual, —the type of paper used and the strength of the toner.

If the toner is fresh a short immersion of 10 seconds may be too much when working with a paper such as Kodalure. In that case, dilute the toner more than is called for in the directions. On the other hand, with the faster chloro-bromide papers, such as Velour Black and Kodabromide, it may take from 30 minutes to one hour to get the tone desired. If in doubt, don't tone too far. Remember—you can repeat the procedure next day after you have seen how the print looks when dried.

Full directions come with each bottle, and I prefer using these "ready made" toners to making up my own. However, if you prefer to compound your own solution, here is a formula which will work:

Selenium Toner for Brown Tones

	Avoirdupois	Metric
Powdered selenium	50 grains	3.4 grams
Sodium sulphide	1¾ ounces	52 grams
Water	16 ounces	500 cc.

The solution should be heated until the selenium dissolves and then diluted to get the tone desired. The less selenium in the toning bath the more toward the sepia the tones will be. If the selenium is precipitated upon dilution, the solution must be filtered or the prints immersed in two separate baths of 1% Sodium sulphide.

Eastman T-21 Formula
Nelson Gold Toner

Stock Solution A	Avoirdupois	Metric
Warm water, about 125° F.	1 gallon	4.0 liters
Hypo	2 pounds	960.0 grams
Ammonium persulphate ..	4 ounces	120.0 grams

Dissolve the hypo completely before adding the Ammonium persulphate. Stir the bath vigorously while adding the latter. If the bath does not turn milky, increase the temperature until it does.

Prepare the following and add it (including precipitate) slowly to the hypo-persulphate solution, while stirring the latter rapidly. *The bath must be cool when these solutions are added together.*

Cold water	2 ounces	64.0 cc.
*Silver Nitrate crystals	75 grains	5.2 grams
Sodium chloride	75 grains	5.2 grams

*The silver nitrate should be dissolved completely before adding the sodium chloride.

Stock Solution B		
Water	8 ounces	250.0 cc.
Gold Chloride	15 grains	1.0 gram

For use add 4 ounces (125 cc.) of solution B slowly to Solution A while stirring the latter rapidly. The bath should not be used until it has become cold and formed a sediment. Then pour off the clear liquid for use.

Pour the clear solution in a tray supported in a water bath and heat to 110° F. (43° C.). During the toning the temperature should be between 100° and 110° F. (38°-43° C.). When desired tone is obtained (5-20 minutes) remove prints.

Dry prints should be soaked before toning and after toning they should be rinsed in cold water and returned to the fixing bath for five minutes. After this they are washed in running water for the normal washing time.

The bath may be strengthened at intervals by the addition of Gold solution B, the quantity depending on the number of prints toned in the bath.

Brown (Sepia) Toning for Bromide Papers

Personally, I rarely use a bromide paper if I later intend to tone it brown. I use bromide papers principally when I want rich, cold blacks. But if you do want to sepia tone a bromide, use the following formula.

Solution A	Avoirdupois	Metric
Potassium ferricyanide ..	1 ounce	30.0 grams
Potassium bromide	1 ounce	30.0 grams
Water	20 ounces	600 cc.

Bleach the print in this solution until every bit of the black has disappeared, then wash it two or three minutes to remove all trace of the bleaching solution. The print must be entirely free from hypo before bleaching or the image will be reduced. The solution keeps well in a dark bottle.

After bleaching and washing, the print is re-developed in:

Stock Solution B

Sodium sulphide	2 ounces	60.0 grams
Water	5 ounces	150 cc.

Take ½ oz. (15 cc.) of stock solution to 10 ounces (300 cc.) of water. Immerse the print in the solution and allow it to develop fully, which should take a very short time. The re-developer should be discarded after use and re-development should be carried out in a well ventilated room.

If the re-developed prints are too light, or reddish, a more pleasing dark-brown tone can often be obtained by only *partially* bleaching the print in solution A. Also, if you add a few drops of 28% ammonia solution to solution A, and also to the *working* solution of solution B, a decidedly darker brown print will be the result.

After the prints are redeveloped, they often will be soft and slippery and should be hardened to prevent frilling, blisters or other damage. They should then be thoroughly washed as usual.

GOLD CHLORIDE BLUE TONER

(See "Blue Toning," page 235)

Stock Solution A	Avoirdupois	Metric
Water	8 ounces	250 cc.
Thiocarbamide	50 grains	3.4 grams

Stock Solution B		
Water	8 ounces	250 cc.
Citric acid	50 grains	3.4 grams

Stock Solution C		
Water	8 ounces	250 cc.
Gold chloride	15 grains	1.0 gram

To use, take one ounce (30 cc.) of each stock solution and add to 10 ounces (300 cc.) of water. This quantity (13 ounces) will tone three 11 x 14 inch prints. The mixed solution will keep for several *hours*. This formula works best with chloride or slow chlorobromide papers and is NOT suitable for bromide papers.

Prints should preferably be well fixed in a plain or acid hypo bath. After a thorough washing, prints may be toned at once or left to dry before toning. Immediately after immersion in the solution, toning will start, and the average print will be toned in about 15 minutes, although it may take as little as 10 minutes or as much as 30 minutes. This will depend upon whether the print was a high or low-key subject and whether it had been developed to brown or black. Dark prints take longer. Keep prints moving while toning. Following the toning, the prints should be washed for one hour.

ACID RINSE FOR PAPERS (STOP BATH)

	Avoirdupois	Metric
Water	32 ounces	1.0 liter
Acetic acid, 28%	1 ounce	30.0 cc.

This bath should *always* be used between developer and hypo unless specifically advised to the contrary. Renew it every hour, or whenever it loses its vinegar-like odor. 28% Acetic acid may be prepared from the glacial form by mixing 3 parts of the concentrated acid with 8 parts of water.

Fixing Baths for Paper

Hypo is usually mixed in a one to four proportion with water, that is, one ounce of hypo to four ounces of water. However, with paper, there is a tremendous amount of latitude allowable for the average paper will fix properly in hypo solutions which may vary from a proportion of 1 to 2 up to 1 to 10. Some papers which bleach readily in the hypo will maintain their quality much better if fixed in a 1 to 10 hypo solution. However, while there are all kinds of fixing baths, the ones listed below will suffice for all types of work. Don't leave the prints in hypo for more than 10 minutes' time. As a final word, it is always best to use two hypo baths, leaving the prints three to five minutes in each, then washing.

Plain Hypo

	Avoirdupois	Metric
Water	64 ounces	2.0 liters
Hypo	16 ounces	480.0 grams

If kept fresh, this formula will fix any print as well as the more complicated formulas. However, it is easily weakened and made useless if developer is carried over into it. The above formula should only be used for one job and not saved for the next day, and the Acetic acid rinse should always be used with it. A plain hypo can fix a print so that it is permanent in 30 seconds! If you use two of these baths and rock the print in each of them for two minutes each, that print would still be good 25 years from now. If you intend to do direct toning, (without heating the toner, and no bleaching) the above formula will give you the most easily obtainable results. It is excellent to use in conjunction with Selenium and Gold chloride toners. One caution, however, it does not harden the emulsion of the print and should not be used during the hot summer months, or with papers which are easily damaged.

Acid Hypo

	Avoirdupois	Metric
Water	64 ounces	2.0 liters
Hypo	16 ounces	480.0 grams
Sodium bisulphite	1½ ounces	45.0 grams

251

(Potassium metabisulphite is interchangeable in equal quantities with the Sodium bisulphite.)

The above is a fine, all-around fixing bath with a certain amount of hardening action. If in doubt use it for all your work, except during the hottest months of the year. It can be used for negatives as well as prints and allows easy toning with direct toners. It will last quite well and can be saved to be used over again.

If the hypo bath begins to show bubbles, or feels slippery, it is time to discard it. Never use hypo about which you have the slightest doubt. Fresh hypo is the cheapest item in photography and one of the most important.

ACID-HARDENER HYPO

KODAK F-5 FIXING BATH

FOR FILMS, PLATES AND PAPERS

	Avoirdupois	Metric
Water, about 125°F. (50°C.)	*20 ounces*	*600 cc.*
Hypo	*8 ounces*	*240.0 grams*
Sodium sulphite,		
(desiccated)	*½ ounce*	*15.0 grams*
Acetic acid, 28%	*1½ fl. ounces*	*48.0 cc.*
Boric acid, crystals	*¼ ounce*	*7.5 grams*
Potassium alum	*½ ounce*	*15.0 grams*
Cold water to make	*32 ounces*	*1.0 liter*

Crystalline boric acid should be used as specified as powdered boric acid dissolves only with great difficulty and its use should be avoided.

This formula is one of the finest hypo solutions if you desire to harden your negatives or prints. It practically will harden any emulsion no matter what has been done to it. I always use it when in trouble with soft or slippery films or papers, and it is best for summer use but not recommended previous to blue toning. Its use may sometimes be necessary *after* blue toning or intensification in order to prevent the print from frilling. If the print or negative has been intensified or bleached and re-developed to sepia, be sure to wash it thoroughly before immersing it in the solution or it may bleach.

Print Hardener

	Avoirdupois	Metric
Water	20 ounces	625 cc.
Formalin	1 ounce	32 cc.

This will help to harden almost any print in from three to five minutes, in the event you did not use a hardener-hypo and hardening is necessary. Don't leave the print in the solution for more than 5 minutes and wash it for 5 minutes after removing it. It is a handy bath to use after toning a print, should the emulsion become slippery and soft, being then liable to damage by sticking to blotters or ferrotype tins. However, this does not have the hardening action of the Kodak F-5 formula, but it does save time in washing.

Cleaner

	Avoirdupois	Metric
Wood alcohol	9¾ ounces	312 cc.
28% Ammonia	¼ ounce	8 cc.

This is a handy solution to have about the darkroom for cleaning glass, condensers, negatives, etc. Tip a bit from the bottle on a soft cloth and let it evaporate a few seconds before wiping the object. Do not apply too wet to films or they may suffer slightly. Especially useful in wiping off specks of emulsion following use of New Coccine.

Water

Water is, of course, the most important chemical we use. Distilled water is always best for photographic purposes but it is comparatively expensive and sometimes difficult to obtain. For ordinary purposes, especially for washing, use tap water or rain water. If in doubt, when mixing developers, either use distilled water or boil the available tap water and let it stand a while until the impurities settle. In New York City, I use the tap water for all purposes except mixing fine grain developers for negative work, when only distilled water is used.

253

PRINT QUALITY QUESTIONNAIRE

One of the most important factors in obtaining print quality is the severity with which YOU *judge your own work. Never submit a print to a client or send it out for exhibition until you have determined that it is the best you can produce. Criticize your own print quality by answering the questions below on each of your prints.*

1. Do I have the proper relationship between highlights, middletones and shadows? Do the negative and paper match as to general contrast?

2. Do I have sufficient separation in the highlights themselves—also in the middletones and even in the shadows? Or isn't it necessary to have this separation in these three distinctive areas?

Most photographers quickly learn the trick of matching negative to print: whether to use soft, normal or contrast grade of paper, but thousands of them forget a very important factor—one of the secrets which gives sparkling print quality, and that is: *local separation, or contrast, should also be present within the highlights, middletones and shadows themselves.*

3. Do I have some real, *pure white* area in the print?

If this pure white area is not present in every print, you will have a muddy result. The print will not be brilliant. However, the area of this pure white, should usually be very small; in a portrait it may be the whites of the eyes or the teeth. In a landscape it may be a few highlights on snow or specular reflections on water, etc.

4. Do I have any real, *pure black area in the print?*

If the print does not have some real black, the print quality will be considered "flat." No matter what grade of paper you use, whether soft, normal or contrast, all of these papers have a range from pure black to pure white and it is your duty to see that each print attains that complete range—whether it is a high- or low-key print.

5. Have I the correct detail in *large* highlighted areas? Do I have the right amount of *texture* in each portion of the print which represents a form or substance?

If you have a piece of cloth or an expanse of snow, have you dodged or printed in sufficiently until those areas show the actual substance of which they are made? Or, do you feel it is not necessary or important to show the texture?

6. Have I darkened the edges and corners of the print so that the picture will be correctly *framed?* Or, is it not necessary?

In most cases you will find it advantageous to "frame" your print in this way.

7. Should this darkening of the edges and corners be done by printing-in?

If it is necessary to bring out a "blocked-up" texture in snow or grass, sky or machinery, you must do your darkening by the printing-in method with the negative in the enlarger.

8. Would it be advantageous to also darken the edges and corners by the "flashing" method?

The flashing method hides or eliminates texture. Be sure that you have learned to distinguish the proper difference in results between *printing-in* and *flashing.* This is extremely important but not always understood. If in doubt, re-read the chapters on printing-in and flashing. In most cases you will find the best results are obtained by a combination of printing-in *through* the negative and then flashing afterward *without* the negative.

INDEX

INDEX Continued